FREELANCE LIKE A PRO

ROSHAN PERERA

Copyright © 2018 Roshan Perera
All rights reserved.

This book is intended for educational purposes and personal use only. You are not allowed to resell, copy, print, share, redistribute, or edit any of the content of this book without proper permission from the author.
All rights belong to Roshan Jerad Perera.
FreelancingHacks.com

Table of Contents

Intro: Who Is This Book For?..1

Who is Roshan?..3

How To Make The Most Of This Book..5

Lesson 1: The #1 Reason Why Most Freelancers Fail................7

Lesson 2: Part Time Or Full Time Freelancing: Here's What To Do...........9

Lesson 3: Preparation - 4 Things To Do Before Starting Your Freelance Career...11

Lesson 4: How To Find Your Marketable Skill.............................14

Lesson 5: Start Building Your Reputation....................................17

Lesson 6: How To Choose The Right Platform To Offer Your Services…22

Freelancing Secret #1 - Build A Quality Portfolio Showcasing Your Best Work...24

Lesson 7: How To Create The Perfect Freelance Profile.........27

Lesson 8: How To Figure Out The Right Price For Your Services...........36

Lesson 9: How To Search and Pick The Perfect Jobs For You...............39

Lesson 10: How To Write The Perfect Client Pitch/Proposal....................43

Exercise 1 - Getting Ready...46

Lesson 11: Avoid These Mistakes When Writing Your Proposal.............47

Freelancing Secret #2 - Find A Brand New Freelance Site To Join.........55

Lesson 12: How To Use Psychology To Influence And Attract More Clients...57

Lesson 13: 5 Things To Ask From Clients Before Accepting The Job......61

Lesson 14: When To Use A Freelance Contract & How To Create One..64

Lesson 15: The Importance Of Gathering Testimonials From Your Clients...68

Freelancing Secret #3 - Don't Be Afraid To Charge More........................70

Lesson 16: How To Avoid Scope Creeps..71

Exercise 2 - Finding Work..73

Lesson 17: How To Beat Veterans And Cheap Freelancers....................74

Lesson 18: How To Ditch UpWork And All Other Freelance Platforms....78

Lesson 19: 10 Quick Ways For Finding Work Outside
Freelance Platforms..81

Freelancing Secret #4 - The One Thing You Can Do To Get Repeat
Clients...88

Lesson 20: How To Write An Effective Cold Email..................................90

Lesson 21: How To Pick And Manage The Right Clients........................93

Exercise 3 - Beyond Freelance Platforms..95

Freelancing Secret #5 - How To Be An Exceptional Freelancer..............96

Invest In Yourself, Your Reputation, And Your Skills..............................98

Epilogue..100

Email Template - For Developers...101

Email Template - For Graphic Designers..102

Email Template - For Marketers...103

Email Template - For Web Designers...104

Email Template - For Writers..105

70+ Websites For Finding Freelance Work..106

10+ Sites For Learning New Skills Online..112

"Your work is going to fill a large part of your life, and the only way to be truly satisfied is to do what you believe is great work. And the only way to do great work is to love what you do. If you haven't found it yet, keep looking. Don't settle. As with all matters of the heart, you'll know when you find it." **- Steve Jobs**

Intro: Who Is This Book For?

Let me get this out of the way real quick. I'm not a millionaire! And I'm certainly not someone claiming to have found a secret formula for making more money as a freelancer.

However, I did managed to make around $5,000 a month working full-time as a freelance writer. It's not something I've achieved overnight. It took me 4 years of trials and errors to get there. I've made a lot of mistakes and failed miserably along the way. But, somehow I made it. So I'd like to think that I know a thing or two about how freelancing works.

As a freelancer, you can never be sure about how much you're going to make next month, no matter how skilled you are or how many repeat clients you have. I'm not saying all this to scare you but only to share a fact that most new freelancers fail to grasp: Freelancing requires hard work!

I see plenty of new freelancers giving up so easily within a few days or a couple months of trying because they somehow seem to believe that free-lancers make money by sitting in front of a computer and clicking on ads or visiting a bunch of websites.

Make no mistake, to be a successful freelancer you'll have to put in a lot of work and practice your craft every day. To do those things every day, you'll need a strong desire to make more money and, more importantly, you'll need a marketable skill with a reasonable demand.

Like most other freelancers out there, I work hard every day. Most days I clock in more work hours than a regular 9-to-5 employee. But, I'm never tired because I love what I do and I don't have plans to retire. Because people only retire when they're "tired" of what they do. Well, not me.

It goes without saying that this is not one of those "get rich quick" books that teach you a bunch of impractical ideas for finding overnight success. Instead the book details some of the lessons I've learned over the years and the strategies that worked well.

To make the book useful to all freelancers, I made sure to include unique tips, strategies, and actionable steps in each lesson in the book. Whether you're complete beginner or an advanced user, there will be something new you can learn in each page of this book.

Get started on reading and enjoy the journey. To make the learning process easier, you can join our exclusive Facebook Group "Freelancing Journey" to ask questions and share your experience along the way.

Who is Roshan?

Let me introduce myself: I'm Roshan Jerad Perera, a freelance writer, blogger, and a web entrepreneur from Sri Lanka. I've been working as my own boss for more seven years and I couldn't be happier.

Before getting started as a freelancer, I worked at several day jobs. The first job I've had was as a lead graphic designer for an advertising agency. Then I went switching from one company to another, doing the same job, for three different agencies before calling it quits.

Truth is I felt miserable working at these jobs. I was never really happy. I always felt as if I'm at the wrong place and that I'm wasting away my time and potential. Then I found an ad on a paper and applied for a freelance writing position at a local technology magazine. I got the job and I worked there for almost 2 years earning less than $5 per article. Then I decided to quit and start my own blog.

Starting my first website, FreshINFOS.com, was a huge deal for me because it's the main reason behind my freelance career. The website didn't make much money with advertising so I had to continue freelancing to cover both the website and living costs.

Elance (now UpWork) is the first site I joined to offer my services as a freelance writer online. At first, I had a tough time making a living as a freelancer. Mostly because I had to work more than what I was paid for.

Along the way, I took a lot of online courses and learned about web development. Then started my own little web design agency with two of my friends. We offered web design services to local clients and also had a few international freelance clients in between.

Unfortunately, the local businesses didn't believe in online marketing, or even having a decent looking website for their business, so our little startup didn't go as well as we had hoped. We ended up shutting down the agency and I came back to doing what I know the best: Writing.

My parents were concerned about my future and the bills were piling up. This time I had no other option but to make it work as a freelance writer. So, I started reading a lot of books, took a bunch of online courses on writing, read all the blog articles I can find to learn more about copywriting, and rebooted my freelance career.

And it worked! After a lot of hard work and hard-learned lessons I now make more money than I ever imagined. And it's all while working from the comfort of my home. I know there are many freelancers out there who struggle to land jobs and make a living working from home. And I also know from experience that asking for help doesn't work well in the freelancing industry because most successful freelancers out there are reluctant to share their strategies.

Which is why I decided to start **FreelancingHacks.com** to share everything I know about freelancing, including my strategies to my freelancing success, with you. Since the beginning of Freelancing Hacks website, I received overwhelmingly positive responses from fellow freelancers. They also sent questions asking for help on how to start freelancing.

I realized that many of these people don't have a proper strategy or a plan to getting started as a freelancer. So, I made it my mission to create a solid actionable plan for all freelancers for finding success.

And the *Freelance Like A Pro* was born.

How To Make The Most Of This Book

One of the most common excuses most people make when starting out as a freelancer is claiming they don't have enough time.

This is why I decided to separate the lessons of the book by 21 chapters to make it easier to digest. All you have to do is read 1 chapter per day and take necessary action that I advise in each chapter.

With this strategy, you can start freelancing even while working at a day job without taking any risks. Of course, I also included some secret tips for growing freelancers sharing some of the tactics that helped me to boost my rates and earn more money as well.

Think of this book as an actionable plan that you can go through step-by-step to get started in freelancing and build a profitable career. And there's no need to quit your day job. At least not yet.

If you're not currently employed, then great. Use your free time to go through this book and get started in freelancing right away. But, if you already have a job and need a stable income to provide for yourself or the family, then don't quit your job yet. You can go through the book and get started in freelancing gradually.

All you have to do is set aside **2 hours** of your day to read this book and follow each step in each lesson every day, for 21 days. By the time you're done with this book, you'll be fully equipped to make some serious money as a freelancer and even be ready to quit your day job to work full-time as a freelancer.

It's crucial that you don't skip any of the lessons in this book. Each lesson in this book is critical for your success as a freelancer. So read the book from the beginning to the end, as thoroughly as possible, and then read it again.

Things You Won't Find In This Book

If you bought this book hoping to find some tricks or methods for fooling the system and scam your way to the top, then stop reading this book right now and go buy yourself a lottery ticket. Because there are no tricks to getting rich overnight as a freelancer.

However, there are so many *hacks* you can use to your advantage. We'll talk more about those later. I wrote this book as a guide that everyone around the world can use get started in freelancing and become a successful freelancer. As a result, I won't be talking about any country-specific laws, Tax, or any other legal matters. You should consult with a lawyer to learn more about it, especially if you live in the US, UK, Europe, or Australia.

Alright, let's get started.

Lesson 1: The #1 Reason Why Most Freelancers Fail

When was the last time you've finished something? You start reading a book, get bored half way, and leave it on the table. Then suddenly you get excited about getting in shape or losing weight, only to start working out and give up after a few weeks.

This is normal. As humans, we get distracted so easily. And of course, let's not forget about procrastination. I'm a big fan of it. You have no idea how long it took me to start writing this page. Oh, look! The trailer for the new Avengers movie is out. Better go check that out on YouTube before start writing. And there goes half of my day.

As I described earlier, I also gave up freelancing after a while because I wasn't making enough money working online. When things got tough, instead of looking for ways to fix the problem, I went ahead and started a web design company. It was just a distraction. Luckily, I got back on track.

It's the same reason why most freelancers fail. You get excited at first and give up halfway when it gets difficult. By purchasing this book, you've made a commitment to succeed. So, I don't want you to do the same mistake most other wannabe-freelancers make.

Don't start freelancing for the wrong reasons. It's not a vacation project for you to earn money while you're on vacation from college. It's not a way to get rich quick.

Think of freelancing as a real job. A job that you'll love doing for the rest of your life. Whether it's writing, web design, software development, or even becoming a remote personal assistant, you must commit yourself totally to succeed as a freelancer. And nothing else.

There will be obstacles, frustrations, you'll have a hard time finding clients, landing jobs, and getting paid. But, be determined to go past those barriers. Why am I telling you all this before we even begin this journey?

Because I want you to develop a strong mindset from day-one. To make yourself want nothing but success. And build a mindset to keep yourself from stopping for anything until you reach your goal of becoming a successful freelancer.

So, ask yourself this: There are thousands of others trying to become successful freelancers. What do you do when thousands of people compete with you for the same thing?

You must **Outwork** them!

Take Action!

Ask yourself this question: Why do I want to be a freelancer?

Take a pen and paper and write down 3 reasons why you want to be a freelancer. Whether it's to finally end the stress of your day job, pay off your debts, follow your passions, or even earn some extra money to support your family, dig deep down and figure out why you choose to become a freelancer.

Stick it on the wall near your computer and read it every day. Imprint those goals in your mind until you want it so badly that you're willing to do anything to achieve it.

For example, it could be something like this: *I Want To Buy A House. I Want To Spend More Time With My Kids. I Want To Do What I Love The Most.*

This may seem ridiculous but do it anyway. It's a proven psychological hack that will help you prime your brain to work harder toward your goals.

Lesson 2: Part Time Or Full Time Freelancing: Here's What To Do

You won't make a lot of money in your first couple of weeks as a freelancer. It takes time to get around the freelancing platforms, learn how to apply for the right jobs, figure out how to get a client's attention, etc.

You need to give yourself some time for all of that. Which is why I always advise anyone who asks me about freelancing to do it part-time at first. Just to get your feet wet and see if you're really up for it.

If you're going to college and looking to make some cash to cover the expenses, try freelancing part time. If you think you're wasting your talents at a meaningless job, try freelancing part-time. If you're a stay-at-home mom who wishes to pay the bills, try freelancing part-time.

Why? Because it's the safest way to get into freelancing without taking a risk. Even if you hate your job right now, don't quit yet. Just set aside 2 hours each day to following the lessons in this book and to work on your freelancing career.

While you're at it, save up some money. My advice is to save up enough money to cover your expenses and bills for 3 months. And then you can safely quit your job with financial security. I guarantee you that if you really work hard and follow the lessons of this book to the letter, all it takes is 3 months for you to get started and make a profitable living as a freelancer.

If you can, work things out with your boss and offer to work for the company remotely as a freelancer. You get to work from home and also gets to work with other clients outside the company while they pay you only for the amount of work you do.

The company won't have to pay for benefits or even a fixed salary. It's a Win-Win situation. Your boss won't be able to resist that deal.

Take Action! - The Best Path To Take

You don't have to give up your day job to become a freelancer. If your paycheck from the day job is enough to cover your expenses, do part-time freelancing to earn a little extra cash without risking going broke.

Go full-time when you feel confident about your skills and have a couple of retainer freelance clients who are giving you jobs on a long-term basis. If you're unemployed, just dive head-on and work even harder than you can.

Building your reputation, finding clients, and making deadlines meet, all this may seem too difficult in the beginning. The challenge is to work past that.

Once you get to the other side, you'll get to experience the full freedom and all the good things that freelancing brings to your life. Just remember not to consider freelancing as a hobby. Think of it as your future career and take it more seriously.

As Vincent Van Gogh said, "great things are done by a series of small things brought together."

Start small, take small steps, but keep your aim high.

Lesson 3: Preparation - 4 Things To Do Before Starting Your Freelance Career

Before we get to the action-packed section of the guide, there are a few things you should do to prepare yourself for the long hard road ahead. You can start by following these tips.

#1 Setup A "Rainy Day" Fund

Why am I keep telling you not to quit your day job right away? Because the chances are it might take a couple of weeks or even months before you earn enough money as a freelancer. And you shouldn't depend on it. At least not right away.

You still have to pay your bills, put food on the table, and provide for your family. So, before you quit your job, start saving up some money in case of a "rainy day".

Get a pen and paper and calculate how much it costs to cover your food and bill expenses for 3 months. And start adding money to your rainy day fund until you have that amount.

While you grow your rainy day fund, you can get started on your freelancing work on the side and work on laying down your initial groundwork. Prepare yourself to face some struggles during this initial phase. It'll be tough, but you can pull it off.

Elon Musk, the billionaire entrepreneur behind Tesla, once put himself to the test to see if has the guts to be successful by living off just $1 dollar per day. Do you have the guts to accept that same challenge?

#2 Improve Your Communication Skills

One of the most important things you need to master to win your clients with your proposals is the art of communication. This means 3 things.

You must:
- Improve your English writing skills.
- Learn to write better emails.

- And learn how to connect with a client on a personal level.

If you need to polish up on your writing skills, take a course on Udemy or EDx.org to learn proper methods for writing without sounding like a corporate drone.

Writing better emails and proposals is the secret to winning your client's heart. I've included some email templates with this book. Study those templates or customize them a little to use them when writing your own proposals.

#3 Create A Schedule For Freelance Work

As I've been saying over and over again, you don't need to give up your day job to start a freelance career. You just need to set aside a couple of hours (minimum 2 hours) each day to work on your freelance gigs.

Instead of binge-watching Game Of Thrones for two hours, use that time to do your freelance work instead. Or finish what you have to do each day, and just go to sleep 2 hours late. You won't have to do this for too long. Once you have enough clients, you can safely quit your day job to become a full-time freelancer. Until then, just work your way up 2-hours per day.

#4 What About A Plan-B?

What happens after I quit my day job? What if I fail as a freelancer? Can I go back to my day job again? Stop right there! Don't even think about a plan-B.

Freelancing works best when you go all-in with everything you've got. That way you'll work harder to achieve your goals because it's the only option you've got. Don't even think about starting this career with an exit strategy. Be willing to face obstacles, overcome failures, and accept nothing but success. Develop that mindset and give your freelancing career all you've got from the very first day.

Take Action!

Get started on these 3 things right now!

- Get get an empty jar and start putting away money to safely quit your job and start freelancing full-time.
- Learn to write well. Read books. Take online courses.
- Get a pen and paper and write your daily schedule. Calculate how many hours you can spend on freelancing each day or which activities you can eliminate to make more free time.

Lesson 4: How To Find Your Marketable Skill

You have to be skilled at something to become a successful freelancer. You may think that anyone can do a job like data entry or social media management, but even those jobs require skills like experience in typing, Microsoft Office, and graphic design.

Don't fool yourself if you think you can scam your way to the top. It will never last and it won't be long before you crash and burn. To build a long-term career, first, find what you're really good at and use it to create your freelance services.

Niche Down, But Find Your Middle Ground

UpWork, the biggest freelancing site on the web, has over 12+ million registered freelancers. And that's just one website. The competition is fierce on these sites. You have to fight hard to land a job on a platform like UpWork or Freelancer.com. If you insist on using these popular sites, the only way to succeed is to find a smaller niche to offer your services.

For example, if you want to offer graphic design services, instead of defining your skill in general as a "graphic designer" choose a niche category like "logo designer" or "infographic designer". This way, you'll have slightly less competition to deal with.

The important thing to remember is to do what you're really good at. For example, as a copywriter, I can handle all types of writing work from website copy to product copy, eBooks and more. But, blogging and article writing is what I'm really good at. I've been focusing my freelance services around this niche and so far it has rewarded me well.

Just remember not to pick a niche that's too small. For example, if you want to find graphic design work and all you can do is design product packaging, then you'll have a tough time landing jobs because there's virtually no market available for product packaging designers in the online freelancing marketplaces.

So, how do you find if your skill is marketable enough to make money?

How To See If Your Skill Is Marketable

There's a simple way you can use to figure out if your skills are marketable enough to make money as a freelancer.

- Go to a popular freelancing website (eg: UpWork.com, Freelancer.om)
- Search for freelance jobs using keywords related to your skillset (eg: logo design)

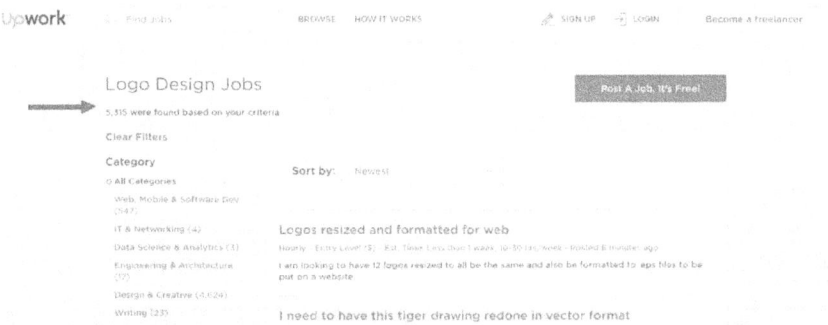

See how many job results come up for your search. If you get at least 500 results for your search, then you have yourself a profitable skill in your hands. Even if it's below 500, you can still make it as a freelancer. But, you'll have to work harder to find clients. My main goal here is to help you get started as easily as possible.

If you want to earn a decent living without having to worry about finding clients at the end of the month, I'd suggest that it's time you work on developing a profitable skill set.

Polish Up Your Skills

When it comes to working online, most of the skills and the experience that you've gathered at your day job or at college may become irrelevant.

I'm not saying that to undermine your knowledge, but things work differently on the Internet. For example, you can't write a blog post the same way you write an essay at college. Blogs use much simpler language with a conversational tone and a technical style article will never get accepted by a blog.

So, polish up your skills before you get started. Follow some online courses to advance your skills or learn new skills from scratch. There are free and premium sites you can use to learn skills online. Don't hold back on investing in your career.

Here are some of my favorite sites for learning online:

- Skillshare.com
- Udemy.com
- edX.org
- Coursera.org
- Treehouse.com

If you don't have any skills yet, don't worry. You can always learn them. But, it will take some time for you to learn and practice your skills to the level of a professional.

And I hate to tell you that you shouldn't continue the next steps in this book if you don't have any skills to offer as services. So, take some time to practice your art and get back to this book once you're confident of your skills and then follow the next steps.

Take Action!

- Dig down and find out what you're really good at doing or what you would love to do for a living.
- Do some research to see if those skills are profitable.
- Take online courses to polish up your skills.
- Practice your skills daily.

Lesson 5: Start Building Your Reputation

Before I started working online as a freelancer, I spent about a year developing my own blog, FreshInfos.com. I wrote daily for this blog on tech-related topics like latest Apple releases, social media, gaming, and others.

When I joined Elance (now known as UpWork) as a freelancer, I was already a seasoned writer with quite a bit of experience and knowledge of everything that's going on online.

This qualification helped me land 3 out of 5 jobs that I pitched to on Elance. Some contractors even contacted me personally via email to hire me for work outside the platform. Just sending them a link to my blog as proof of my writing skills was enough to get invited to a whole lot of jobs every week.

Needless to say, establishing your background and reputation is one of the most crucial factors of finding success as a freelancer.

My website and the experience I gained writing thousands of blog posts certainly helped me land a lot of clients. And you can use the same technique to attract more clients too.

The best part is you don't have to spend years developing your own blog because there are plenty of well-established websites that already allow you to publish your articles for free. This is called guest blogging.

What Is Guest Blogging?

Guest blogging is a strategy you can use to gain free publicity. You write an article on behalf of a website, in return they will publish it for you for free with an author byline with links to your personal website and social media pages.

Here's how the process works:

- You contact a reputable blog that accepts guest posts, like Huffington Post or Entrepreneur.com
- Pitch your idea for a great blog post to publish on their site.
- Once you get their approval, send your article with an author byline explaining what you do and links to your social media profiles.

As a freelancer, you can use guest blogging to get more exposure for your services and also use it as examples of your work.

How It Helps Build Your Reputation

Most freelancers who pitch for jobs on sites like Upwork and Freelancer.com doesn't have any credible experience or proof of their work. This obviously leads to lower success rates and bidding wars.

If you can take the time to at least publish 3 or 4 guest articles on a few reputable websites, you will have an incredible advantage over the rest of the cheap and demeaning freelancers who are just waiting for clients to fall out of the sky. So the next time when a client asks to see examples of your previous work, you can simply send them a link to your article published on Huffington Post, which will knock their socks off.

Believe it or not, even some of the millionaire entrepreneurs like Richard Branson, Mark Cuban, Bill Gates, and Neil Patel often publish guest posts on popular websites to gain more exposure for their businesses and products.

So why shouldn't you use the same trick to double your earnings?

How to Get Approved by A Great Website

Getting approved by these popular websites is not going to be easy because they receive guest blogging requests from bloggers every day. The trick is to write a pitch focusing on how the blogger can profit from your article and suggest a unique article idea that they can't resist.

More importantly, don't write your email to these sites like a robot. Get personal. Find the name of the person in charge and address them by their first name.

My freshinfos.com website received over a dozen guest blogging requests per week and I ignored most of them because some emails sound too robotic. I could tell that they were just copy-pasting the same email template over and over. As if they have sent the same email to 100 other websites. So, don't make the same mistake.

What About Programmers, Web Designers, And Other Freelancers?

Guest blogging is a great strategy to build reputation and awareness not just for freelance writers, but also for other types of freelancers including designers, coders, and marketers. There are different kinds of blogs out there, all you have to do is find a blog that's relevant to your industry and submit a blog post.

Also, there are other ways to build your reputation. For example, if you're a web designer, you can design a free website template and release it online to get more exposure. If you're a graphic designer, you can use a site like Behance to build your portfolio.

If you're a coder, you can contribute to an open-source project on GitHub.

4 Ways To Build Your Online Presence

Even if you haven't got a freelance gig yet, you can start building your reputation right away. In fact, I would highly recommend that you build your online presence before you create a profile on a freelancing site.

Here are a few ways you can do that.

Start A Blog

The easiest way to build a name for yourself is to build your own blog and start writing about the things that promote your work. For example, if you're a web designer, you can write about the HTML frameworks you use for designing websites. Or write case studies on the projects you've worked in the past.

Not only your blog will help you to get discovered by new clients, you can also use it as a proof of experience when you pitch to clients through freelance sites. You can build a blog for less than $100 using WordPress. Or you can start a blog for free on a platform like Medium.com.

Get Published On Another Blog

Getting published on an established blog is another great way to build your reputation quickly, especially for freelance copywriters and marketers.

Find a blog that relates to your industry and contact them to ask if they accept guest posts. Pitch your idea and then you can send them your post to publish with your author byline. For example, if you're a freelance graphic designer, you can reach out to a blog like Design Shack to publish a guest post.

Here's a list of over 300 websites that accept guest posts (https://solvid.co.uk/180-websites-that-accept-guest-posts/).

Do Free Work

Most veteran freelancers will always advise you against doing free work. But, when starting new, you need to develop proof of work to present to your potential clients as examples of your skills.

Here's a trick I used to build reputation as a web designer when I was promoting my web design agency:

- First, I browsed Google Play and Steam store looking for game and app developers who didn't have a website.

- I sent them an email explaining why they need a website and offering to do it for free.
- A few companies responded back and I made them awesome websites. With my name and link to my personal website on the footer (eg: designed by Roshan Perera).

Then I used those sites in my portfolio to showcase as proof of my skills. You can use a similar strategy to get your name out there. You don't have to do the jobs on freelance sites for free.

Challenge Yourself

Challenging yourself to do something remarkable and documenting it is another cool way to build a reputation for your work.

A designer named Peter Majarich did the same when he challenged himself to design a movie poster every day for 365 days. As a result, he was featured on multiple design blogs and his work went viral on social networks.

It doesn't take a genius to figure out that he must have gotten a ton of job offers after this incredible challenge. Don't set limits for yourself by the standards set by others. Find your own unique ways to set yourself apart from the rest. Show how remarkable your work really is and give your clients a reason to hire you instead of the others.

Take Action!

Get started on building reputation for your work. Find a way to make a name for yourself and a way to show off your skills.

- Start a blog. Publish a guest post. Or release a free website template.
- Do a personal challenge or find your own way to stand out from the rest.

Lesson 6: How To Choose The Right Platform To Offer Your Services

UpWork, Freelancer, PeoplePerHour, Fiverr, these are the most common sites freelancers first sign up when starting their career. Don't make that mistake. Avoid these sites at all costs!

Just because these sites are popular and have more job listings doesn't mean you have a higher chance at landing more clients. It's actually the opposite. Popular sites like UpWork are filled with millions of freelancers who compete with each other to land jobs. In fact, some freelancers even use bots to automatically post a proposal to every new job posted under certain keywords.

Others demean themselves by falling for bidding wars, in which the freelancers offer lower prices than the project budget hoping to outbid the other to win the client. This is why I decided to quit using these major platforms like UpWork. It just wasn't worth the effort.

Which Site Should You Sign Up?

While I encourage you to avoid major freelance platforms, every new freelancer has to start somewhere so a freelance marketplace with low competition is probably the best way to find your first job as a freelancer.

UpWork and Freelancer aren't the only websites available for finding freelance gigs. There are hundreds of others. Find a site that's fairly new and become an early adopter. Create your profile on this site. When you're one of the first few freelancers to join a site, you have a higher chance at landing a job.

I've included a massive list of freelance sites and job boards with this book. You'll find plenty of new freelance sites in there. I guarantee you'll find a job from at least one of these sites.

Quality, Not Quantity

You might think that registering on a bunch of freelance sites and applying to every job you can find is a good strategy to improve your success rate, but it really isn't. When you try to multi-task and apply to a lot of jobs, you will have to sacrifice the quality of your proposals.

Writing a killer proposal is the key to landing a client. And in order to write the perfect proposal, you have to spend a lot of time researching about the client, reading their job descriptions, and crafting a pitch that they can't refuse. You can't do this time-consuming process for 50 times per day.

Try to focus on finding jobs from a couple of freelance websites. This will help you narrow your focus and develop a high-quality freelance profile. Which will improve your chances of getting more ratings and reviews for your profile. Or you can avoid freelance marketplaces and use job boards.

Stick To Job Boards

Freelance job boards let you apply to jobs without having to register a profile, worry about ratings, or compete in bidding wars with other freelancers. When using job boards, you can contact a client directly via email and send them a pitch to discuss the job. Also, when using job boards, you don't have to pay a platform fee and lose money.

A great example of a job board is the ProBlogger Jobs board. This is like the go-to jobs board many freelance writers (myself included) use to find work. And it's always filled with high-paying jobs.

You'll find a list of job boards in the freelance sites list included with the book.

Take Action!

Visit the freelance sites I've included with this book and browse the jobs posted on those sites. Pick 2 or 3 sites that you feel comfortable with. Bookmark them for later.

Freelancing Secret #1 - Build A Quality Portfolio Showcasing Your Best Work

After writing a proposal for a job and sending it to a client, one of the first things that the client is going to ask in reply is a link to your portfolio.

A portfolio is a website you can use to neatly showcase all your best work in one place. While it's not required for a freelancer to have a portfolio, it will greatly improve your chances of convincing the client that you're a professional. You can create a portfolio in many different ways.

For Web Designers & Developers

Welcome home, developers

GitHub is home to the world's largest community of developers and their projects...

If you're a web designer or a developer, you can design a unique personal website and showcase some of the websites you've designed for clients. If you don't have any client websites to showcase, then go do some free/paid work.

Once you've done some work, you can build your portfolio. You'll have to buy a domain name but you can get free hosting from a free Github account or from OpenShift. I can't go into detail on how to create a website for free. Just try Googling how to create a website with GitHub to find a step by step guide. If you have spare cash, you can buy hosting to build your own website as well.

Web developers can also use a site like CodePen and GitHub to share their code snippets and plugins while also using your profile as a portfolio. In fact, if you're a coder, most clients will often ask to see your GitHub commits profile to see the projects you've worked on.

There are plenty of open source projects on GitHub. Find a few you can contribute to.

For Graphic Designers

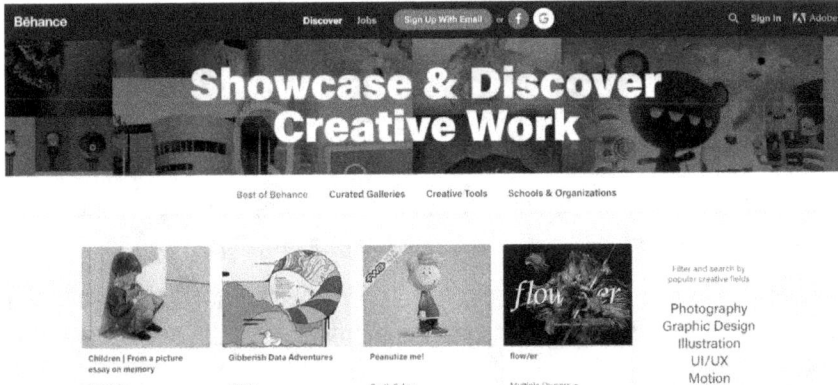

Graphic designers can build their portfolio on a platform like Dribbble or Behance. Getting into Dribbble is not easy. You'll need an invite from an existing user to get into the platform. And they are not easy to come by.

Behance is easy to join. It's free and it's already filled with thousands of freelance designers. You can use your Behance page to share your designs and even get more exposure.

For Writers and Others

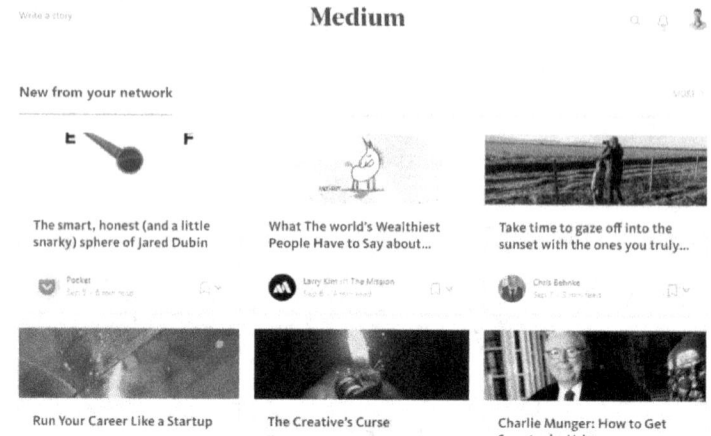

For writers, having a few links to some of your previously published articles is enough to convince a client that you're a pro.

While a portfolio website is not completely necessary for a writer to pitch to a client, having a blog can greatly improve your chances of winning over the client.

Start a self-hosted WordPress blog if you can. Or use a platform like Medium.com to blog about the topics you love and the industry you're working in. You can also contact an established blog and ask them to write free articles for them as a contributor. In return, ask them to mention that you're a freelancer for hire in your author byline.

This will not only help you land clients, the process will also help polish up your skills. While this may not seem like a big secret to you, having a portfolio could be the one thing that could help improve your success rate of landing clients.

As I've told you earlier, having my own blog made it easier for me to convince clients of my writing skills. And that's is what got me to where I am today.

Lesson 7: How To Create The Perfect Freelance Profile

Having an incomplete freelancer profile or a profile with poor copy is one of the main reasons why most freelancers have a hard time landing clients on platforms like UpWork.

Because when you apply for a job on a freelance platform, the first thing your client do is checking your profile to learn more about you. And an incomplete or a bad profile might give your clients the wrong impression of you.

If you're serious about making a career as a freelancer, the first thing you need to do is create a complete and an attractive freelance profile.

Using UpWork as an example, I'll show you what kind of features you need to include to create a complete freelancer profile on any freelancing site. Of course, you can apply these same methods with other freelance platforms as well.

#1 Use Your Real Name

Even though it's common sense to use a real name when doing business, many freelancers use fake names on their freelancer profiles.

Don't be ashamed of your true identity. Don't be afraid to use your real name on your freelancer profile no matter how difficult it is to pronounce. It will help you stand out. Your name doesn't have to sound cool or common. There are too many John's and Jane's out there. We don't need more!

Also, avoid abbreviating your name (eg: John S. or Amy C.). Use your first and last names, for god sakes! If you're afraid of exposing your true identity, you don't belong in the freelancing industry.

#2 Upload A Professional Photo

Don't even think about using a selfie or a really weird close-up webcam photo as your profile picture. That's a mistake most amateur freelancers make.

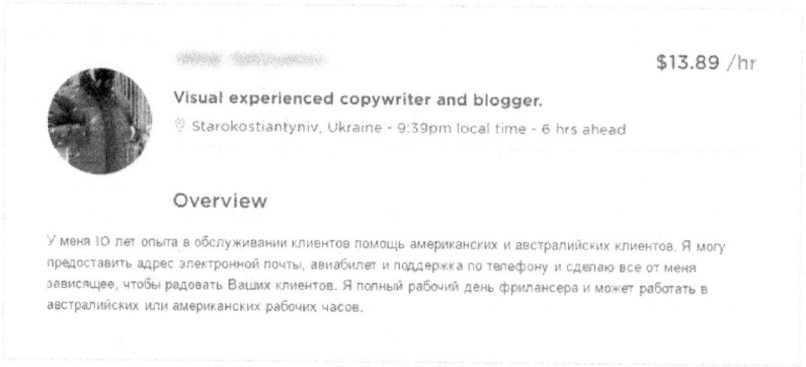

Get cleaned up. Dress well. And ask someone else to take your picture. Make sure not to give too much attention to the background. More importantly, SMILE!

Did you know that smiling not only makes you more attractive and look confident, but studies have found that it also increases your chances of getting promoted in your job.

If you can, go to a studio and get a photograph taken by a professional. It'll be worth it.

#3 Craft A Specific Headline

Your headline should describe your job title. So, try to be as specific as possible to make it easier for your client to understand what you do.

No, not like that. This is not Twitter. Use a more professional headline

For example, if you're skilled in writing eBooks then describe yourself as an "eBook Writer", instead of just "Writer". Or "WordPress Plugin Developer", instead of "Web Developer".

Narrow it down to a niche and you'll have a better chance at getting discovered on a big platform like UpWork.

#4 Write Your Bio In First-Person

Don't describe yourself in third-person like you're narrating a movie and avoid writing your freelance profile as if it's a page on a corporate website.

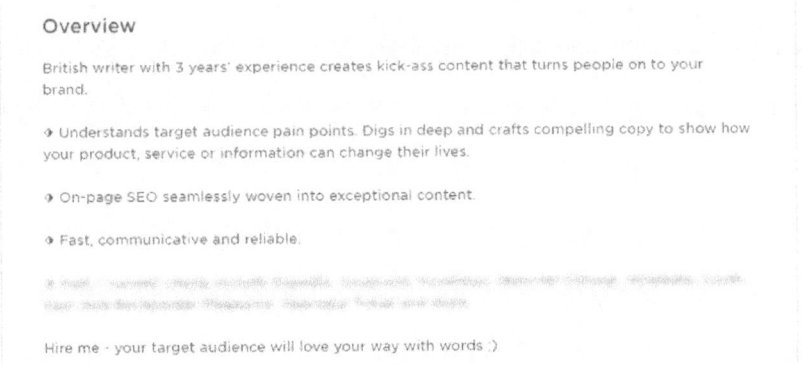

See what I mean. Did you enjoy reading that description?

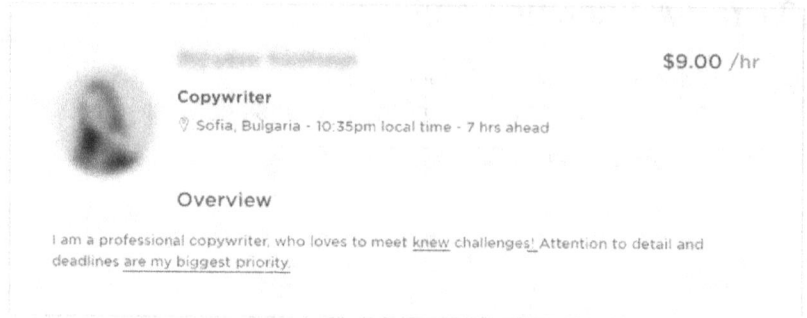

And take a look at this. See what's wrong here? Does this person sound like a professional copywriter?

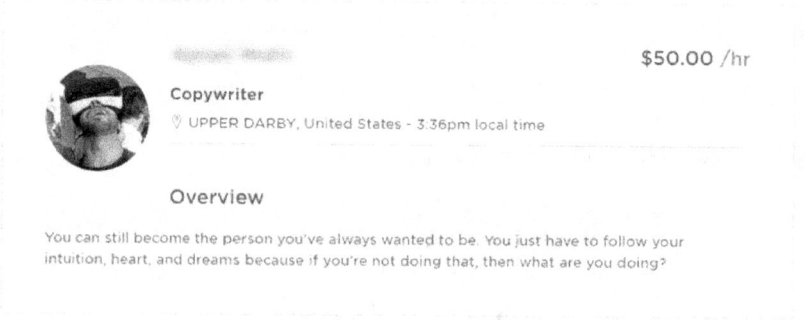

Yes, this one's a real profile too.

Instead, what I want you to do is to get personal. Imagine that you're writing this bio to send it to an acquaintance. Not a close friend or a hiring manager, but someone who doesn't know you very well.

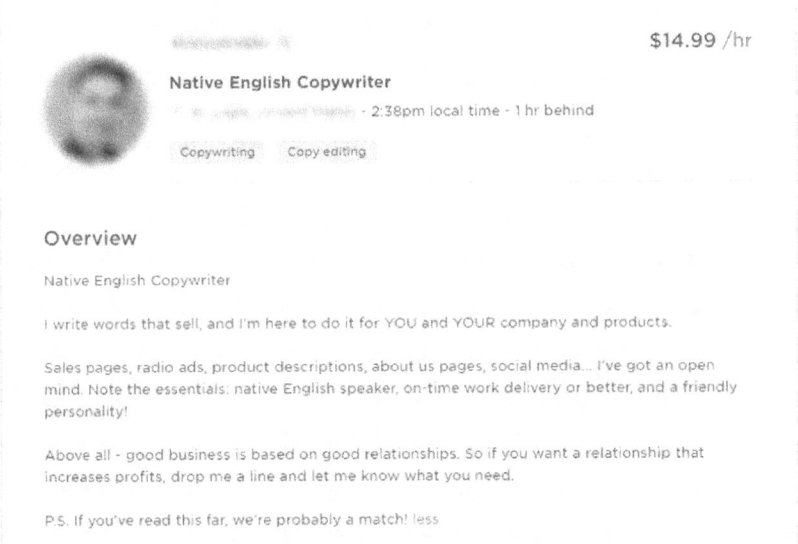

Something like this.

I wouldn't call that the perfect bio, but it's efficient. And I must admit that last postscript made me laugh.

Your clients aren't interested in your hobbies or your life goals. So, keep those personal details to a minimum. You're creating a freelancer profile, not an online dating profile. And try to keep the description below 200 words.

#5 Describe Your Qualifications And Experience

It's best to include a sentence or two about your qualifications and experience in your bio. But, try not to brag too much. Don't be this guy.

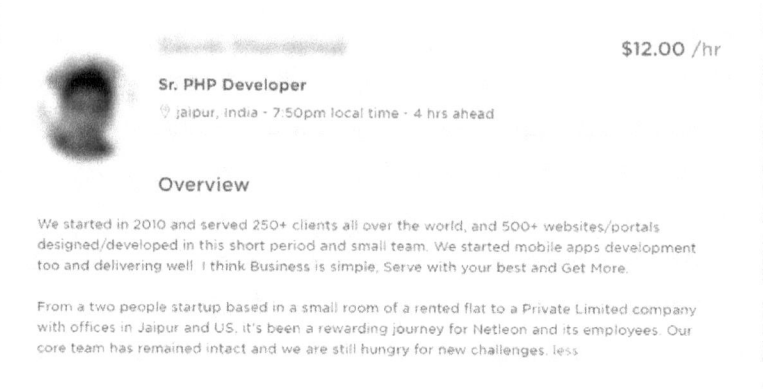

Also, use the "Employment History," "Education," and the "Other Experiences" sections to add more personality to your profile.

#6 Showcase Your Best Work In The Portfolio

UpWork and many other freelance sites give you separate sections in your profile for showcasing your portfolio. Use it well to show off your best projects.

Upload an attractive image, write a detailed description of the project, and include a link to the source. If you're trying to create a profile on a different platform that doesn't have portfolio section, use a site like Behance.net to upload your work and simply include links in your freelancer profile bio.

#7 Connect Your Social Networks

Freelance sites also let you connect your social networks and portfolios with your freelancer profile.

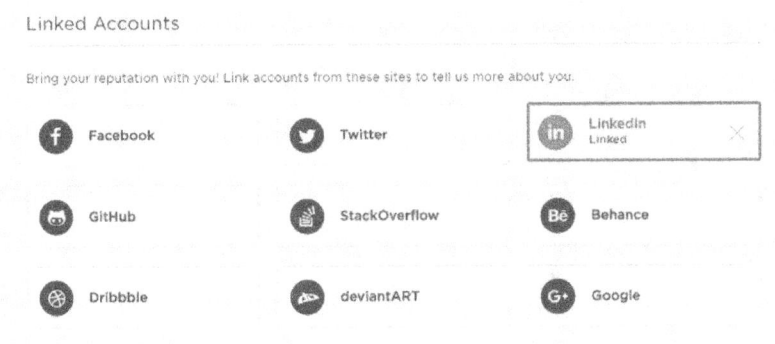

Even though the links to your social profiles won't be shown to your clients, it's important that you connect at least a couple of your social profiles with the platform as it helps the sites to better understand you to create a more personalized experience and to show more relevant jobs in the "Find Work" section.

#8 Skill Tests Aren't Important But Take Them If You Can

"The more relevant tests you pass, the more professional you look" At least that's what UpWork says on the website. But, it doesn't matter how many tests you pass on UpWork. Clients couldn't care less about these tests because these tests are no match for real hard work.

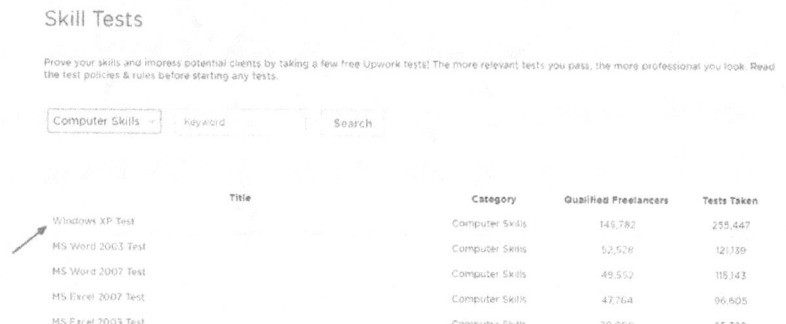

A skill test in Windows XP? Is this 2001? As long as you have a solid portfolio to show off your reputation you shouldn't worry about taking any tests. But, feel free to take as many tests as you can, if you have the time.

A Few More Tips For Going Forward

- **Run A Spell and Grammar Check:** Use a tool like_Grammarly_to check your profile bio for any errors before making it public. It will only take a few seconds to save yourself from a huge embarrassment.

- **Steal It:** If you can't figure out what to write in your description or even how to write it, check out some of the successful freelancer profiles to get an idea.

- **Ask For Reviews:** Most clients will immediately leave a review once a job is complete, but don't be afraid to ask for a review if they didn't.

- **Ask For Referrals:** If your client says you did a great job, then ask them to refer you to other clients. There's no shame in asking for a referral or help.

- **Add A Video:** UpWork now allows you to include a video in your freelancer profile. This is a great way to attract more attention to your profile. But, not mandatory.

Remember, your freelance profile is your online CV. So, don't make it too personal. Forget about your hipster styles, selfies, and emojis. Be professional, or try to act like one. Now, go wow your clients with your amazing profile.

Take Action!

Sign up with the freelance sites you picked from the list and create a complete profile that attracts and win new clients.

Lesson 8: How To Figure Out The Right Price For Your Services

One of the most difficult things most freelancers struggle with in the beginning is figuring out the right price for their services. While there's no perfect strategy for finding the ideal price, there are a few "unorthodox" methods you can use to find the right price for your services.

Method 1: Find What Others Are Charging

Explore freelance marketplaces and find out what kind of prices others are charging. Take a piece of paper and write down how much freelancers are charging based on their experience.

For example, if you were to visit PeoplePerHour, you can browse its freelancers according to category and see how much they are charging. In this case, software developers on this platform are charging various prices from $20 per hour to $66 per hour. You'll also notice how their prices differentiate based on their country.

Using this data, you can try and find a number that's suitable for your level of skills to price your services. In addition, you can use tools like Glassdoor Salary Calculator and Bonsai's Freelance Rate Explorer to find out what others are charging.

Method 2: Pretend To Be A Client

For freelancers who don't use hourly pricing, finding the perfect fixed price for a project can be challenging. Because different projects come in various sizes.

An easy way to solve that problem is to ask from another established freelancer in your field. Of course, they won't share their pricing details with another freelancer. So, what you can do is pretend to be a client and reach out to them. Ask for a quote on a made up project and see how they price their projects.

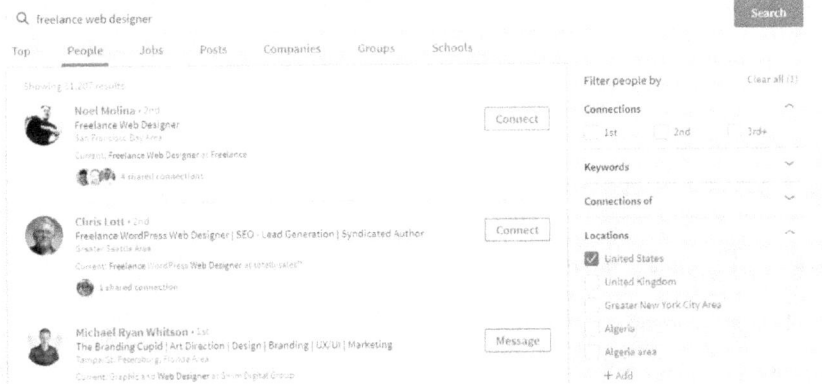

For example, if you're a freelance web designer, go to LinkedIn and do a quick search for web designers. They usually have their personal portfolio websites linked to the account. Find their email and send a message.

Method 3: The 3X Method

Begin by creating an expense budget for your monthly costs. Find out how much you'll need to cover your monthly expenses or whatever financial goal you're planning to achieve by freelancing. Then, multiply that total by 3X. Now, divide the outcome by the total number of hours you can work per month.

For example, if you can work 8 hours per day every work week. Then you'll have 160 work hours every month. Let's imagine that you need $1,000 per month to cover the costs of your bills and food.

$1,000 X 3 = $3,000.

Divide that $3,000 by 160 hours and you'll get $18.75 per hour.

> 8 hours per day X 5 days a week
> = 40 hours per week
> 40 hours X 4 weeks = 160 hours
>
> $3,000 / 160 = $18.75

That means if you charge $18.75 per hour, you'll be able to reach 3 times the amount of your financial goal. Why 3X? Well, you have to account for your availability. Work won't be available for you all the time.

Keep Experimenting

As I've mentioned in the beginning, there's no perfect strategy to find the exact right price for your services. It differs based on the level of your skillset and experience.

When I first started freelancing, I charged $5 for a 1,000 words article. After over 7 years of slow progress, I now charge over $90 for writing the same type of article. So, try starting with a price that you believe is fair for both you and your client. Start from there and slowly work your way up the ladder. Keep experimenting and increasing your price as you gain experience.

Take Action!

Before applying for a job, make sure you know what you're worth. Find out the right price to charge from your clients without overcharging or appearing cheap. Go do the research.

Lesson 9: How To Search and Pick The Perfect Jobs For You

Not all jobs on freelance platforms are worth your time and effort. There will be jobs posted by terrible clients who will squeeze you for every last drop of sweat to get the most amount of work out of you. And of course there are clients seeking free work as well.

You shouldn't waste your time negotiating with clients who will ask you to do free work or scope creeps who try to squeeze a ton of work out of you before making the payment. It's crucial that you learn to find the right jobs that fit your skill set.

How exactly do you do that? Let's find out.

Separating The Good From The Bad

Again, I'll show you how to spot the good clients from the bad using Up-Work as an example. Let's imagine that I'm a web designer looking for a simple design job. Now, let's go look for a web design job. I'll just enter "website design" into the search bar and see what comes up. Now, this is a solid job that I might want to apply.

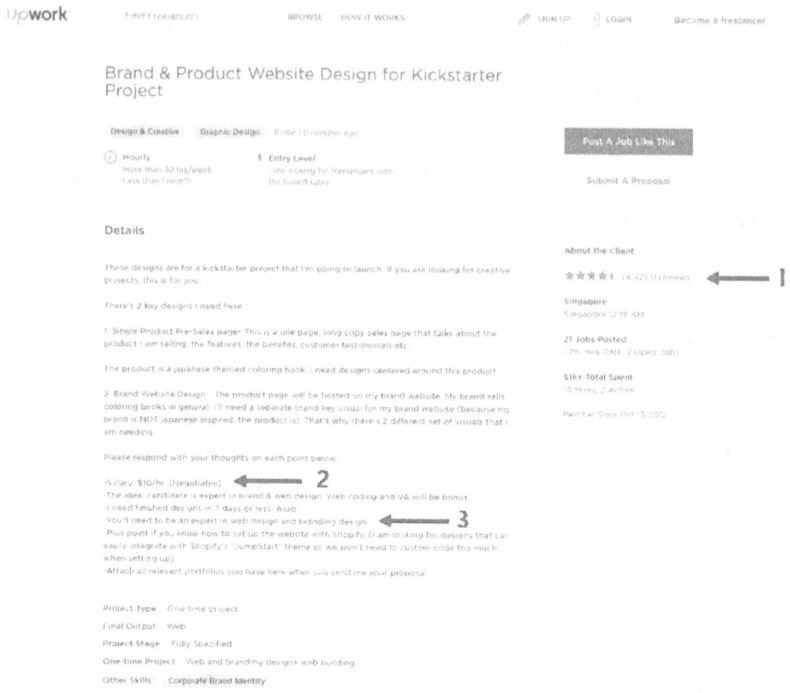

1. First thing I did was check the client's profile. Seems like he's posted jobs before and out of the 16 freelancers who's worked with this client, 11 have left good reviews. Which means the client can be trusted.

2. Then, I checked the budget for the project. Website designs require a lot of work and improvements. And this client offers to pay on an hourly basis and the rates are negotiable as well. That's a good sign that shows this client is not a scope creep.

3. The client is also very specific about the project details and mentions in the project brief what exactly he wants as the outcome. This shows promise that the client wouldn't settle for less or cheap freelancers.

So, if you're a good web designer with a solid portfolio, applying to this job will improve your chances of landing the client.

Let's see what kind of jobs you might want to avoid. Like this particular job which showed very suspicious signs.

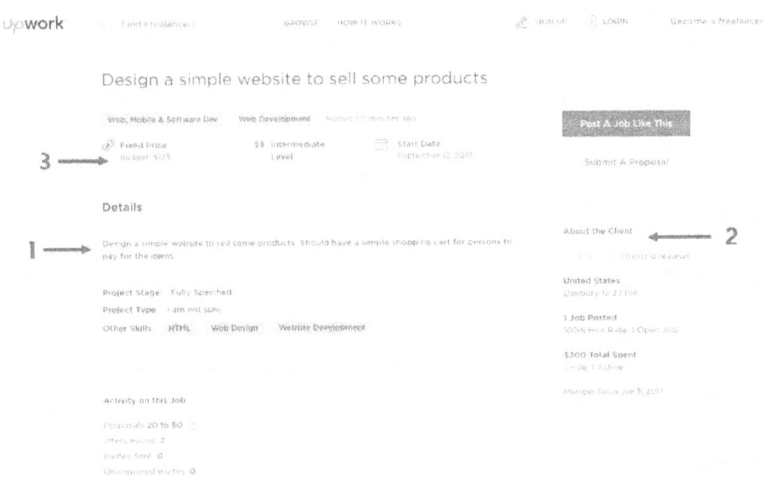

1. First, the title is undefined and the description is too short. What type of product is he plan on selling? Does he want a WordPress store or a Shopify store? What type of shopping cart system does he want?
2. Next, you can see the client is new to UpWork. Which means the chances of you running into trouble is pretty high.
3. The budget is also alarming. $125 for a website design is way too low. And from the looks of the short description, this job will require a lot of work to build a website with a shopping cart system.

You can still apply for this job. But, the client will more likely award this job to the cheapest freelancer and that freelancer will end up doing way more work than what he signed up for.

Use Gigs As Stepping Stones

Keep in mind that each client you pick for a job will be a stepping stone for your career. You can start with a simple website design project and move on to designing a corporate website and then to a web app.

Try to find jobs that challenge you to step out of your comfort zone. If you stick to doing what you're only good at, you'll be no better than those ordinary people stuck at cubicles working on a dead end job. Focus on using each gig you apply to advance your career, one freelance gig at a time.

Take Action!

Instead of applying for jobs at random, pick jobs carefully. Choose the ones that help you grow. And learn to spot bad clients. Carefully study the jobs posted by clients and learn how to pick a good job that fits your skills.

In the next section, I'll show you how to write a great proposal.

Lesson 10: How To Write The Perfect Client Pitch/Proposal

The client proposal is the message or the email you send to your clients when applying to their job listing. This is the message that you'll use to explain why the client should hire you for the job.

Needless to say, this is the most important part of landing a job. The first impression you make on your client matters a lot and it will play a major role in whether you'll get approved or not.

Tips For Writing Better Proposals

Whether you're applying for a job on a freelancing site or sending a proposal to a client directly via email, here are a few tips you can follow to make your proposal more effective.

#1 Use A Clear Subject Line: Always get straight to the point with your subject line. Try to keep it short. For example, "Regarding Your Craigslist Ad" or "Application For Copywriter Position". Notice how I capitalized the first letter of all words to grab more attention.

#2 Use Proper Formatting: Break your proposal message into smaller paragraphs. Use bullet points whenever you can. This will make you look more professional and make the message easier to read.

#3 Don't Send To Multiple Recipients: When applying to multiple jobs via email, avoid sending the same email to all clients at once. Adding multiple recipients to your email means that you will be modifying the content of the email for a group instead of an individual. Personalizing your email is important for connecting with your client. The same applies when sending proposals via freelance marketplaces. Never copy paste the same proposal twice.

#4 Address By Name: Do your best to find out at least the first name of your client or the person in charge of hiring. Address your client by their first name and spell it correctly when writing your proposal. "A person's name is to that person the sweetest and most important sound," says Dale Carnegie.

#5 Include Your Signature: At the bottom of your email, include your full name, your title, and links to your social network profiles and portfolio websites. Use an email signature when applying via email. You can use HubSpot's email signature generator tool to create an HTML email signature.

#6 Following Up: Don't send too many follow up emails. It will make you seem desperate and the client will eventually mark your emails as spam. Wait at least a 3 days before sending a follow-up email. If landing this client is really important for you, then send another follow-up email after a 3 more days. If you don't get a response after that, it's time to move on.

#7 Double Check Your Message: Proofread your message twice before sending it. Use a tool like Grammarly to check for spelling and grammatical errors.

Using these tips, you can write a simple and attractive proposal.

Here's an example proposal you can use -:

> Hi [Client's name],
>
> My name is [your name] and I'm a freelance copywriter.
>
> I just saw that you're looking for a blog article writer for your business blog and I think I can help with your project. Here's why.
>
> I've been working online as a freelance writer for [number of years] years and I managed to help develop several great and successful blogs for my clients.
>
> Not to brag, but I also have multiple articles published on popular authoritative websites such as [mention and link to the websites]. Have a look and see if my writing style fits your blog's audience.
>
> I understand that getting a lot of shares on social media is just as important as optimizing articles for search engines. And I use a handful of tools to make sure to optimize content for both those areas.
>
> If you like, I can come up with some topics and ideas for great articles for your blog.
>
> Kind regards,
>
> [Your email signature]

I've included 5 different email templates with this book. You can use them when applying for jobs. There are templates for web designers, copywriters, graphic designers, marketers, and developers. You can use the emails as inspiration and create your own versions of proposals when applying for jobs

Take Action!

Practice writing better proposals. Try sending a proposal to a client today!

Exercise 1 - Getting Ready

Test what you've learned so far.

Q1: How many hours are you willing to work every day on freelance projects? What can you remove from your schedule to free up more time?

Answer:

Q2: What is your marketable skill?

Answer:

Q3: How do plan on building your reputation?

Answer:

Q4: Which freelance platforms did you pick to offer your services?

Answer:

Q5: How much do you plan on charging for your services?

Answer:

Lesson 11: Avoid These Mistakes When Writing Your Proposal

Many freelancers complain that even when they have a portfolio and a great profile on a freelance site, they still fail to land jobs from clients. The main reason for this is they make common mistakes that make them appear as amateurs or unprofessional.

To find out what kind of mistakes freelancers make, I decided to go undercover and do a small case study of my own. Here's what happened.

My Own Little Experiment

For this case study, I chose the two biggest freelance platforms on the web, Freelancer.com and UpWork. I signed up with each platform as a client and posted two different jobs on each platform:

1. A web design job for developing a real estate website
2. A content writing job for a business blog.

The four job listings I've posted on both sites received a total of **228 bid proposals** from various freelancers.

Main Takeaways Of The Experiment

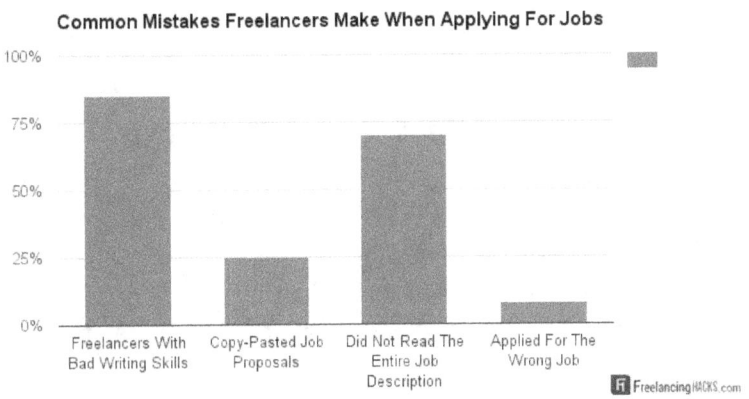

- **85% of freelancers have bad writing skills** - About 190 bid proposals were poorly written and contained bad grammar. I actually had to read them two or three times just to understand what they were saying.
- **Freelancers on *Freelancer.com* are more competitive** - Within only 60 seconds of publishing a job on Freelancer.com, I received proposals from over 30 freelancers almost instantly. It was clear that they were using bots to apply for jobs.
- **Competition in freelance Web Design is tough** - On both UpWork and Freelancer.com, the web design job I posted received the fastest and the most bid proposals.
- ***UpWork* is a slightly better platform for quality freelancers** - Almost all the best proposals I've received were from UpWork and they also lived up to their qualifications as well.

Lesson 1: 7 Out Of 10 Freelancers Didn't Read The Full Description

In each job I posted on both Freelancer.com and UpWork, I included a special keyword at the end of the description asking the applicants to mention that keyword in their proposals to confirm that they've read my entire description.

> Please include the keyword "EXPERT" in the top of your proposal to clarify that you've read the entire description.

This is a trick most freelance clients use to save their time when reviewing freelancer proposals and to quickly find the freelancers who didn't even take the time to read the description of the job. As it turns out, those clients were right.

Most freelancers who applied for my job listings didn't include the keyword. Which means they didn't even care enough to read the full description.

Solution: Understanding the requirements of the job is important for not only writing the perfect pitch, but also to provide the best services you possibly can. Forget about other competitive freelancers for a second and take time to read the description of the job to learn what kind of a freelancer the client is looking for.

Lesson 2: Copy-Pasting Proposals Don't Fool Anybody

As I've mentioned earlier, I received a lot of proposals for the jobs I posted on Freelancer.com within the first minute of posting the job listing.

Nobody can read the long description I included in the job and write a detailed proposal at the same time within 30-seconds.

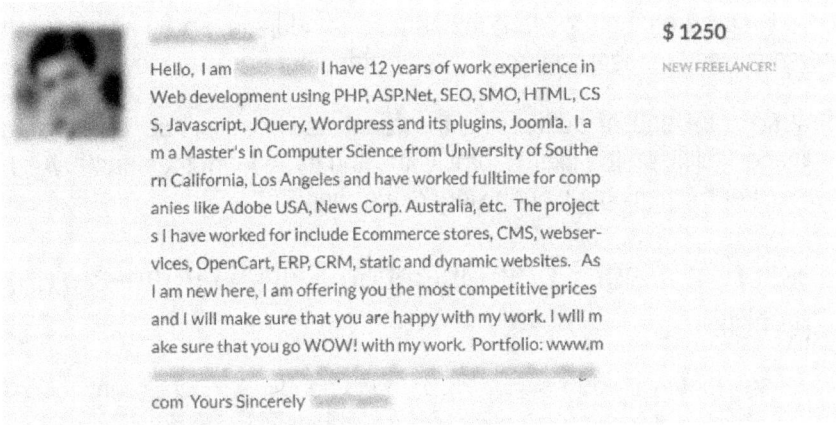

Don't take your client for an idiot. I could see right away that you've assumed the job requirements by just reading the title and copy-pasted a proposal template from another job.

Solution: I understand, the competition is tough and you must try to be the first to send a proposal to a job. But clients aren't in a rush to pick a freelancer for their job right away. You have all the time in the world. So, what's the rush?

Lesson 3: Learn More About Your Client Before Applying

I used an alias for posting the jobs. The name I used was Mike Ford, which was clearly visible in both username and the client profile. But none of the freelancers even bothered to use that first name to address me.

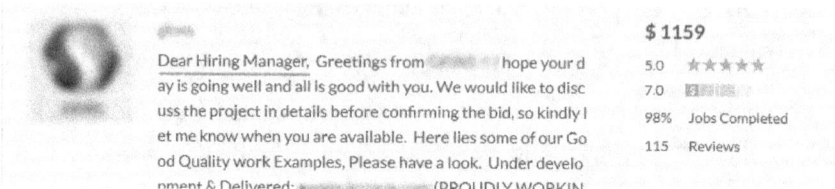

Every time I receive an email or a message from someone addressing me by my first name, I always send them a reply. Why? Because I know this person cared enough to learn my name and address me by my name. It personalizes the message and makes it stand out from the crowd.

Solution: Instead of addressing the client as "Dear sir" or "Dear hiring manager", click on the client's profile link and try to learn their name. Also, remember to check the work history of the client.

Lesson 4: Poor Communication Skills Damages Your Credibility

It doesn't matter if you have a Ph.D. in Computer Science, client's won't trust or believe what you're saying if your writing skills are poor.

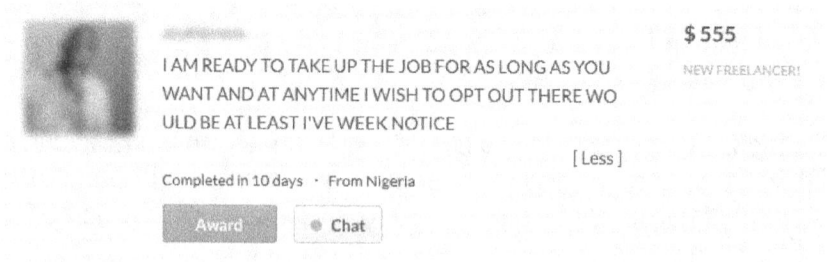

For some reason, this freelancer thought that using all-caps in his message would convince me to pay more attention to his proposal.

Solution: Learn to write better emails and proposals without sounding like a corporate drone. There are plenty of online courses available on sites like Udemy.com and edX.org on English language and copywriting. Take one or two courses and learn to build strong relationships with clients.

Lesson 5: Most Freelancers Apply For The Wrong Job

Many freelancers (around 8% to be exact) had no idea what they were doing. Just take a look at the proposals I received for website design and copywriting job listings.

```
Overview

Working on web development since from 3 years.I have also worked on many live
projects of sharepoint 2013.which are mostly from UAE.

I have worked on many web application ,I also focuse on QA and quialty of work.my
first prioirty is to deliver a quailty work.
following are the my expertise.
c#,
asp.net
html 5
jquery
javascript
Linq
Sql server
Entity framework
Mvc
```

Believe it or not, this is a proposal I received for the copywriting job. In the description, I specifically mentioned that I'm looking for a copywriter to write blog posts about marketing, real estate, and social media. I have no idea how "expertise" in web development can help this person write blog posts for my real-estate business blog.

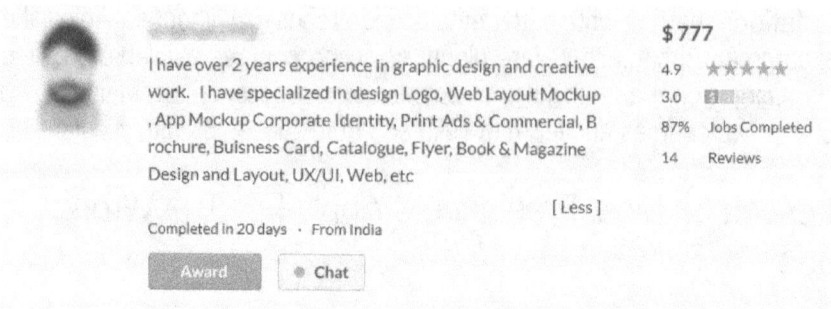

This designer thought he was applying for a graphic design job when the freelance project description clearly states it's a job for a website developer.

Want to see a great proposal? See how this freelancer wrote an intriguing proposal while giving me advice on how to approach the job and even coming up with a possible time frame for completing the project.

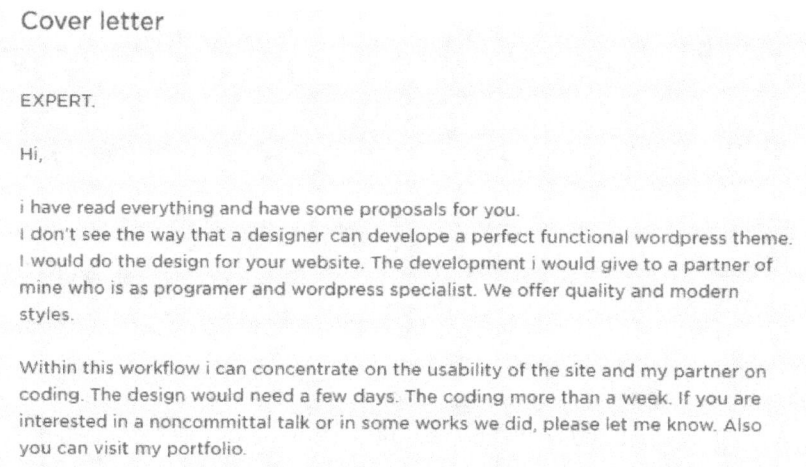

Solution: Focus on applying for the projects that you can truly contribute to, instead of applying to all the jobs that show up on your website feed.

Lesson 6: Bad Profile Photos Shows Bad Personality

Only a few freelancers were using real-life photos as their profile pictures. Even those photos were horrible. Some were using their passport photos and selfies while the others looked like they were plotting to kill me.

Your clients will often judge your personality by the looks. So, it's best to show a smiling personality in your profile photos.

"I think that anybody that smiles automatically looks better." - Diane Lane

Solution: Avoid using logos, drawings, illustrations, fake stock photos, or selfies as your profile picture. Grab your smartphone and ask a friend to take a decent photo of you while smiling. Use it in your freelance profile.

Lesson 7: Bragging Too Much Ruins Your Reputation

Take a look at how this freelancer goes on and on about her interests, education, and skills for the entire cover letter.

> Cover letter
>
> BLOGGER
>
> I have a lots of interest in writing blogs on different kind of topics.My objective as a Blogger is to participate in educational forums and social networking platforms and deliver sound commentaries, unbiased opinions and non-destructive views. Having been in this industry for over two years, I have largely contributed in meeting corporate objectives through effective blogging, thereby driving traffic to their websites and increasing their web visitors. I am very educated in creating web contents, blog feedback, and knowledgeable in ,HTML,advertising,facebook, and Adsense concepts. I also possess excellent communication and wide vocabulary skills. With this said, I am very confident that I will be good blogger for you requirements,

If you look closer, you'll notice how she's made a few writing and grammar mistakes while bragging about her writing skills. The irony.

Instead of bragging, what you should consider doing is providing solutions to your clients. No client likes to work with a "know-it-all". They look for someone who understands their requirements and do work as they ask you to do.

Solution: Limit your bragging to one or two sentences, at most. Use the rest of the space to explain your approach to the job and how you can provide a better service.

Lesson 8: Charging Way Too Low Makes You Look Cheap

I priced the website design job at between $750 - $1,500. I was surprised to see how many freelancers tried to get the job by lowering their prices. This one freelancer said he would develop the entire website for just $400.

```
                                                    $750
Expert And I will do it within $400 Anyway, I am an experien    5.0      ★★★★★
ced web and mobile developer. Here are few sites that I have    2.9
created. I am only sending you best ones instead of huge list,  100%  Jobs Completed
I can share with you more websites if you are interested in lo  3     Reviews
oking into what I have done or you can see my portfolio at htt
...
or1/portfolio/ Looking forward to hear from you soon. Than
k you,
```

Why would you lower your price to $400 when the client offers a minimum $750?

This is what bidding on freelance sites all about. It only goes to show that you're either an imposter who knows nothing about the website design. Or someone who's too desperate to land a job.

Solution: Proposing a bid too low will only reflect on your skills and the quality of your work. But, that doesn't mean you get to ask whatever price that comes to your mind either. Simply try to use a system to figure out the price based on the difficulty, skills, your experience, and the time it takes to complete the project.

If you can keep these points in mind when writing job proposals, you will greatly improve your chances of landing the job.

Take Action!

Don't make the same mistakes other freelancers make. Take their mistakes as lessons and learn from them.

Freelancing Secret #2 - Find A Brand New Freelance Site To Join

When I first started freelancing online I had no idea what I was doing. I had no one to get advice from and other freelancers I reached out to had no interested in networking. It was frustrating because even when I had skills and a good portfolio I still had to compete with cheap freelancers who would offer to do a job for a lower price.

This is still the biggest problem with major freelancing sites like UpWork and Freelancer. These sites currently have millions of freelancers and it's not easy to compete against established freelancers who already have profiles filled with 5-star reviews and others who offer lower prices just to land the job.

My First Big Breakthrough

I was barely making enough money to pay the bills and I had a tough time landing jobs most of the time because I was asking higher prices than other freelancers. Considering my experience in blogging, I knew I was asking the right price but there's always a cheap client who outbids to win the client. This struggle went on for more than 4 years. Then something amazing happened.

I came across a blog post that announced a brand new freelancing site. A site called Envato Studio was opening a new copywriters section on their platform. And they were inviting freelancers to join.

Envato Studio only accepts established and skilled freelancers who already have a solid background. It was kind of intimidating but I gave it a try. I submitted my application and got accepted. Within two weeks, I landed my first job on the platform. And it was worth more than $500. I've never made that much money before in a single project. Ever since that day, I've been receiving job offers from many clients. Even via email.

You see when I published articles on client blogs I included by author bio with a link to my Twitter. I had a link to my portfolio website on my Twitter. So, the clients who liked my articles managed to find my email and contacted me for job offers.

I'm no longer using any platforms to find work but I still have that profile I made on Envato Studio. Because making the decision to join Envato Studio was my first big breakthrough.

Be Smart, Don't Compete

Why was I successful on this new platform when I could barely make any money on UpWork? Well, there's a reason for that.

I was one of the very first few freelancers to join the copywriters section of Envato Studio. And I had a killer portfolio when I already joined the platform. So, when a client came to the site looking for a copywriter, I had very little competition. And it immediately made my success rate of landing clients jump through the roof. If you ever wondered the secret to my success, this is it!

And this is exactly why I always encourage you to find new freelance sites with low competition to join. Because it's easier to land jobs on those sites. In addition, always keep an eye out for fresh new freelancing sites. There are new freelancing sites launching all the time these days. It will give you the edge you need to get ahead in your freelancing journey.

Create a Google Alert for keywords like "new freelance site" so that you can get notified whenever a blog or a news website announces a new platform.

Lesson 12: How To Use Psychology To Influence And Attract More Clients

Ever since I read the book Methods of Persuasion by Nick Kolenda I've been fascinated by psychology. I found many more books on the topic and I read so much about this subject. As it turns out, our subconscious mind can be easily persuaded and manipulated by things all around us. The good news is, there is a way to take advantage of it to do things we want.

According to researchers at the University of Rochester, our unconscious mind is the driver behind our conscious mind.

"You don't consciously decide to stop at a red light or steer around an obstacle in the road. Once we started looking at the decisions our brains make without our knowledge, we found that they almost always reach the right decision, given the information they had to work with."

It's our unconscious mind that steers us to make the best decisions. And as many studies, books, and research have shown, we can manipulate our subconscious mind for our own good as well.

Now, I'm not saying that you should use psychology to scam clients. Not at all! But, there's no harm in trying a few simple tricks to influence your clients.

Make Your Prices More Attractive

Imagine you're in a bookstore looking for a textbook.

There are three different books: A 160-page book for $5, a 250-page book for $7, and a 300-page book for $10. Which book would you buy? You would go for the $7 book, right?

It's more likely for anyone to choose the 250-page book because people have a tendency to compare before making choices. In this case, the $7 option seemed like a good bargain compared to the others. This is why most of the time you choose the medium pizza or medium popcorn.

What if you applied this same technique to your freelance pricing to stand out from other freelancers? I'm not telling you to lower your rates. Not at all. That would have a negative effect and clients would think that you're a fraud if you price your services cheaper.

However, you can use the psychology of pricing to beat your competitors and stand out from the rest of the freelancers. For instance, if a different freelancer offers to design a Logo for $50, you can offer to create a Logo plus a free mockup design for $50.

It's the same price, but with added value.

Persuade Clients To Give You The Job

Followings are statements from two different freelancers. If you're looking to hire one of them, which one would you pick?

Freelancer #1 – "So far, I've designed over 30 websites for major brands and I run my own web design agency, but I only have one year of experience."

Freelancer #2 – "I only have one year of experience, but so far I've designed over 30 websites for major brands and I run my own web design agency."

Both these statements contain the same words with only a slight adjustment in the word arrangement. But, the statement of the Freelancer #2 sounds more confident and trustworthy because it doesn't end on a negative thought.

Remember to avoid making the mistake of explaining your skills first and your weaknesses later. The arrangement of your words in your pitch can make a big difference. Use strong Power words in your pitch that evoke positive emotions, like success, free, unique, instantly, and effective. Just be careful not to oversell yourself.

Show Off Authority

A client is more likely to hire a freelancer with 100 positive feedback reviews than a freelancer with 5 reviews. No matter which freelance platform you choose, do everything you can to build your authority on the platform.

Ask your clients to leave reviews, show screenshots of the websites you've designed, include links and names of the blogs you've been published.

Even if you're a complete beginner, if you could get one of your articles published on Huffington Post or a get your website design featured on Awwwards, you won't have to try and convince your clients of your expertise. Your work will do that for you.

Exude Confidence

"I think I can do this job. If you can give me the job I will try to do my best."

What do you think of that statement? Do you think this person is confident about his skills and abilities? Would you ask him to design a high profile brand logo or a website?

No one would waste their time and money on someone who "thinks" he can or wants to "try" a job. Confidence is the key to building trust.

Having a strong character with a little bit of ego will help any freelancer to grab the attention of their clients and increase their chances of getting approved each time they send a pitch.

Say YES first, you can figure it out later.

The Reverse Psychology Effect

Clients receive pitches from freelancers begging to get approved all the time. I saw plenty of them in my case study. Sometimes, playing hard to get is the best way to get a client's attention. Because even though we are all grown up, we still want that thing we can't have.

The reverse psychology is the effect that makes you want something even more when you know you can't have it.

Strangely enough, this has happened to me on several occasions. When I get offers from clients I sometimes reject the jobs that aren't suitable for me. Saying "NO" to these clients simply makes them want to hire me more.

It's strange because I would redirect them to other freelancers who are more suited for that type of jobs or I would reject them saying I have zero experience in that field, but they keep asking me to take the job.

Give this trick a try when you feel comfortable. Don't try it with all your clients just try it when you're comfortable with your skills and experience. Being confident in your skills and authority is the key to pulling it off. Just give the client a hint that you have better offers and that you're careful about saving your time for better jobs.

Take Action!

Take notes. Practice. And learn to optimize your job proposals and emails with psychology tricks to prime your clients into giving you the job.

Lesson 13: 5 Things To Ask From Clients Before Accepting The Job

Landing a client is an amazing feeling. You get an immediate boost in confidence and you feel invincible like you're Superman. But, don't let that excitement cloud your judgment. When you get a reply from a potential client saying that they would like to hire you, always send a reply with a bunch of questions.

The only way you can avoid any confusion is by properly understanding the project you're about to accept. So, make sure you ask these questions from your clients before accepting the project.

#1 What Is This Project About, Exactly?

In the freelancing industry, there is a type of clients called "Scope Creeps". These clients are like vampires looking to suck your blood until they get the most for their money. They will send you a simple description for the job asking you to do some simple tasks. And then while you're in the middle of the project, they will add additional tasks to the project asking you to do more work. Or sometimes even ask you to do free work to test your skills.

Understanding the scope of the project is crucial to avoiding scope creeps. So, ask as many questions as you can to learn more about what kind of a result the client is looking for. Ask them to show you an example of the outcome they're expecting. For example, if the client wants a website designed, ask them to show a website with a similar design to what they're expecting. That way you'll be able to get a basic understanding of how much work you'll have to put in for the project.

#2 What Is The Project Deadline?

As a freelancer, you'll be working with multiple clients at a time. This means you will have to schedule different amounts of time for each client. Always ask what kind of a deadline the client has before accepting the project. If the deadline seems a bit too short for you, then ask if they're flexible on the deadline.

This will give you more room to work on projects without having work 24 hours a day.

#3 What Kind Of Knowledge Should I have?

Most freelancers should always ask this question.

Many clients will always look for additional skills outside your basic skillset. For example, when working with a business blog, I'm often asked to format and upload my articles to their blog via WordPress. This requires knowledge of using WordPress admin dashboard.

Web designers will have to learn about web hosting and using FTP clients. Graphic designers will need to be able to work with different vector and raster graphic editors.

Asking what kind of work the project involves will help you get a head start and maybe learn those extra skills while you're on the job. If you'd don't know about something, just don't say NO. Say YES, and learn to do it on the job.

#4 How Will You Pay Me?

PayPal still doesn't fully support every country, including mine. As a result, I'm not able to receive payments via PayPal. This has cost me a lot of jobs over the years because most clients who get in contact with me only use PayPal to make payments.

Even if you don't have any issues with PayPal, always ask your clients how they're going to pay you, when the payment will be made, and which payment method they're using. It's best to ask the questions before it's too late.

Also, try asking your client for an advanced payment. Like a deposit for the project, especially if it's a large project that's going to last for a long time.

#5 Are You Willing To Pay For Revisions?

When I write an article for a client I offer to do 2 revisions for free. This means if the client asks me to change something after delivering the article, I will do it for free, twice.

However, if a client comes to me asking to change an article too many times. Or update an eBook that I've delivered months ago, that's where I draw a line. That accounts for extra work and I always charge for that kind of work.

It doesn't matter if you're a complete beginner, you should never do work for free (unless you're building reputation). Make it clear about how much work you're willing to do for the project and mention how many revisions you're offering for free. Let them know that any future updates will count as extra work.

This will save you a lot of arguments, in case something goes wrong. These are the main questions that you should always ask from your clients before accepting a job.

Of course, there are many other questions you can ask. Like if you need to sign any contracts, how often you should update the client on progress, and even ask follow up questions after delivering a job, such as how the project went, if they liked your work, or even if they would keep you in mind for future gigs.

Take Action!

Don't be too quick to accept a job. Understand what the client needs by asking questions. Draw boundaries to avoid problems. And be willing to learn the extra skills that the job requires.

Lesson 14: When To Use A Freelance Contract & How To Create One

I've been freelancing for many years and so far I haven't signed a single freelance contract agreement. One time, I had to sign a nondisclosure agreement but that was it. That's the beauty of working with international clients online. There's no need for signing documents, contract agreements, or deal with lawyers if you know you can trust your client.

Of course, it's not the case for most other freelancers, especially for those of you who work with local clients. For those freelancers, a contract agreement is a must-have. But, you don't need contracts for each and every client you work with. For example, if one of your previous clients offer you a new job, you shouldn't have to sign another contract since you already trust this person.

If there's a need for signing a contract, here are a few things you should consider.

What Is A Freelance Contract?

A contract is a legal agreement between two (or more) parties where they agree on an arrangement. Which, if necessary, can be used in court as proof to defend yourself.

It doesn't necessarily mean that a contract gives you the power to take your clients to court when they avoid paying you, even though there have been many cases of such.

It can be used that way too, but the main purpose of a freelance contract is to have a properly organized document where you detail the scope of the project you're going to work on and what kind of work you'll be doing and won't be doing.

"Contract law is essentially a defensive scorched-earth battleground where the constant question is, "if my business partner was possessed by a brain-eating monster from beyond spacetime tomorrow, what is the worst thing they could do to me?" - Charles Stross, award-winning author.

Simply put, you create a freelance contract to have something solid to refer to when clients try to ask you work outside the scope of the project or when they try to change the project into something entirely different than what you agreed upon.

Do You Really Need A Contract?

If you, like most freelancers, use emails to discuss the projects with your clients, agree on rates, deadlines, etc, then there's really no need for a separate contract at all.

That's right! An email is a contract. An email discussion between you and your client where you exchange promises and agree upon certain conditions is a contract. You don't need another document written by a lawyer to feel safe. If you're working with international clients, you can use your email thread as your contract.

However, if you're working with local clients, having a legally binding contract agreement written down on paper makes sense. For example, if you're a web designer who works with local clients, a contract will help you make things clear to your clients that after you finish the design of the website they will pay you or you will take them to court.

As Seth Godin puts it in his Freelancer Course on Udemy.com, this is only important when working with one-time clients. When working with the same client over the months or years, sending an email with your scope of the project is more than enough.

What To Include In A Freelance Contract

If you don't feel safe sticking to emails, you might as well go ahead and create your own contract. But, contracts and taxes are two of the subjects that I often try to avoid when giving advice to freelancers because different countries have different rules and laws.

So, while I strongly advise you to go to a lawyer for creating bullet-proof contract agreements, there are a few things you must always include in your contracts. These are also known as contract clauses.

1. **Basic Information:** Names, addresses, and all the basic information of all the people involved in the contract.

2. **The Scope of the Project:** A clear and precise outline of the project and the work you'll be doing. Also, mention how much you'll be charging for work outside the scope.

3. **Revisions:** Explain how many free revisions you'll be offering and how much you charge for extra revisions.

4. **Pricing:** Make your prices or hourly rates clear to your client. Explain your charges for additional work too.

5. **Deadlines and Cancellations:** Describe when you plan to deliver or how you'll be paid for your work if the client decides to cancel the project (also known as Termination Clause).

6. **Copyrights and Ownership:** Depending on the type of work you're doing, this section will describe who owns your work after you delivered and if the client will hold the copyright.

7. **Choice of Law Clause:** This is the section where you and your client agree to go to court in case of disagreements of disputes.

Keep in mind that these are only the basics of a contract outline. Some contracts require more detailed sections and clauses. An average contract can be as lengthy as 6 to 10 pages.

How To Create A Freelance Contract

If you're not keen on taking advice from a lawyer (which I recommend), it's important that you at least seek advice from someone who understands the laws in your country before crafting a contract.

However, if your goal is to get a simple freelance contract to cover the scope of the project, then you can create a basic contract by yourself. Your contract doesn't have to contain a ton of technical paragraphs that nobody cares to read. Just write it down the way you understand it and keep it simple and friendly. You wouldn't want to sound too forceful and scare your client away.

Contracts aren't overrated. They have their uses. But, you don't need them for each and every client you work with.

Frankly, if you've been dealing with too many bad clients or scope creeps, it's time you take matters into your own hands and craft a good contract agreement as a strong backup system. Asking your client to sign a contract doesn't make you a jerk, it's a great way to show integrity and professionalism. Just know how to ask it without irritating your client.

Take Action!

An email discussion can be considered a valid contract. But, it's always good to protect yourself from bad clients. So, create a contract suitable for your work. Keep it ready for when you apply for a job outside a freelance platform.

Lesson 15: The Importance Of Gathering Testimonials From Your Clients

Seth Godin is a legend in the freelancing community. He's been a freelancer for decades and inspired many to choose it as a career. Seth tells a great story on the importance of testimonials in his online course for freelancers. It goes like this.

One day, the heating system of Seth's house breaks down. He contact several technicians to come to his house and give him a quote on how much it would cost to fix it. After many disappointments, one person catches Seth's attention. This one technician comes to Seth's house bearing a book filled with testimonials from other clients he's worked with before.

He hand this book to Seth and asked to read the testimonials while he checks the heating system. This was a fresh experience to Seth and, of course, he hires this man on the spot.

The moral of this story is that your claims alone of having worked with big brands and clients are not enough to convince a new client of your skills and abilities. You'll also need proof. That's why you should start collecting testimonials from your clients from the very first day you start working as a freelancer.

How To Collect Testimonials

Now, if you're working with a client through a freelance platform, it's easier to get them to write a review about your service and leave a rating on your profile.

Back when I was working from Envato Studio, I would always ask every client to review my service after delivering a job. This helped me rank at the top of the platform.

But, if you're working with clients directly via email and outside freelance platforms, you can still ask for testimonials and feature them on your portfolio website. If you work with a lot of short-term clients you can use a simple Google Form to create a client feedback form to make it easier for the clients to write a testimonial.

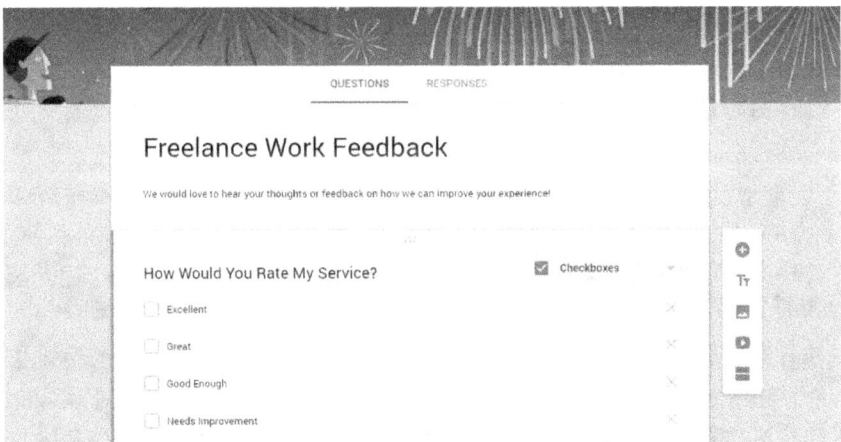

Clients always get cheaper offers. There will always be someone who's willing to do work for a dollar less. But, experienced clients know how much it costs to hire a cheap freelancer than paying extra for a professional who gets the job done in the first try.

Your client testimonials will help convince your new clients to make the right decision and pick the safest and proven effective choice: Which is you!

Take Action!

Setup a system to collect testimonials from your clients. Feature the best testimonials on your portfolio or personal website. Always show these testimonials to your new clients.

Freelancing Secret #3 - Don't Be Afraid To Charge More

I've lost count on how many times I've changed my pricing. When I first joined Envato Studio, I charged $25 to write a blog post. After a few months, I bumped it up to $30. And then $35. $40. And to $50. And guess what? Clients kept ordering my service despite the change in price.

Truth be told, changing the price is scary. The first time around, I actually went back to my old price thinking clients won't order my service. But then I held my ground and maintained the price. I'm no longer working on Envato Studio and now I charge over $90 per an article.

There are many US-based native English freelance writers who charge even less than my price. But, I managed to beat them, even while learning English as my second language.

What's the secret? Don't be afraid to charge more!

I used to be afraid to ask for more because I feared the clients would turn me down. This is a common problem on freelancing platforms as well. Which is one of the reasons I no longer look for work on freelance sites.

Try This Simple Strategy

A good rule of thumb would be to figure out your price and add an extra 10-25% to your price when pitching to clients. If the client agrees, then great! If she says the price is too high, you can offer a discount by going to your original price. It's a win-win kind of a deal.

Just remember, as the years go by your experience and skills will improve. This means your price can improve as well.

Know your worth and charge for it!

Lesson 16: How To Avoid Scope Creeps

A common issue most new freelancers come across when working online is having to deal with clients who try to get you to do work for free or make you do more work than you first agreed. These people are called scope creeps. These greedy clients will keep adding more tasks to the project to make you work beyond the scope of the project without paying for that extra work.

Avoid them at all costs!

Say NO To Free Work

If a client asks you to write a blog post, design a graphic, or mockup a website for free, just to test your skills, always say NO!

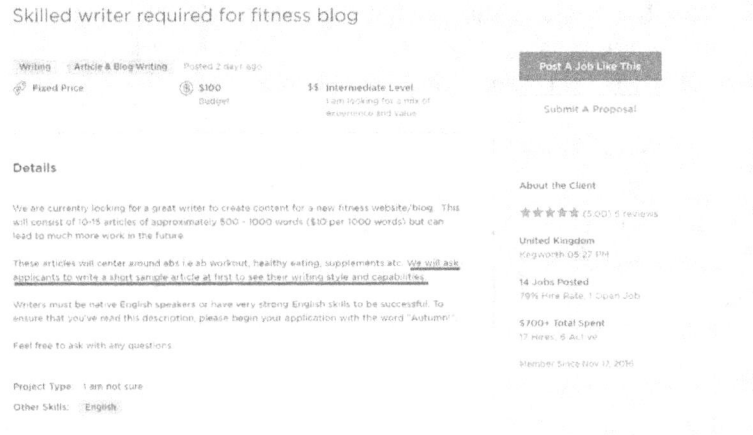

Most clients are confident enough to mention it in their job descriptions and it's the easiest way to spot a scope creep.

If a client wants to test your skills and abilities, they will pay for your work. Whether it's a test run or not, you are sacrificing your work hours to do the work. You deserve to be paid. Don't be afraid to ask for payment if the client insists on a test.

Imagine if you apply to 3 jobs per day and end up doing free test work for each of them. You won't have time to do any actual work.

Keep A Limit On Revisions

Every project you work on will require some amount of updates, unless you can create flawless masterpieces in the first take. The clients will always come back to you asking to change something or add something to the project. These are called revisions.

There are some clients who would keep asking you to change things over and over. That's their way of making you do more work for free. To keep these scope creeps at bay, always specify how many revisions you're willing to do on the project before you start.

Understand Client's Vision

If you can understand what kind of an outcome the client is expecting, then you'll be able to avoid any misunderstandings in the future.

Be sure to ask a lot of questions to make sure you understand the client's vision. And also ask to see examples to get a proper idea about how the project needs to be done.

Use A Project Management App

Project management apps, like Trello and Asana, allows you to streamline your entire project by breaking it down into smaller tasks. Then you can setup a time schedule for completing each task. This will allow you to determine how much work you're going to do and how much time goes into the project.

Add your client to your Trello or Asana project page and let them see your plan for the project. It will also help you keep your clients updated on your progress from day-one. This way, they won't be able to come back to you and ask for additional work without paying you for it.

Take Action!

Say NO to free work and free test work. Always ask your worth for tests. Since you already have proof of your work, you shouldn't have to do trials at all.

Learn to avoid bad clients. Sign up with Trello or Asana to use them to streamline your projects like a true professional.

Exercise 2 - Finding Work

Test what you've learned so far.

Q1: Which job would you pick: 1- $500 for one month project. 2- 350 per month project for three months?

Answer:

Q2: When is the right time to send a follow-up email?

Answer:

Q3: Why should you find brand new freelance sites to join?

Answer:

Q4: Name 3 questions you should ask from your clients before accepting a job.

Answer:

Lesson 17: How To Beat Veterans And Cheap Freelancers

When you're starting out as a beginner, it's always tough to land jobs on freelance platforms. Because most clients usually go with the veterans, the most experienced freelancers who has lots of 5-star ratings. Don't let this define your freelance career. It's still possible for you to land a job while beating the other veterans and cheap freelancers. Here's how.

Method #1: Build Your Reputation

"Hi, I'm a freelance writer, blogger, and the founder of FreshInfos.com. I've been blogging for over 4 years and I've been published in multiple online publications. Links to my recently published articles are below"

This used to be my opening line when applying for jobs on Elance (now UpWork).

Most other freelancers never stood a chance against my pitch because my reputation made me stand out of the crowd. If you're a freelance writer, get an article published in Forbes. If you're a web designer, design a website for a startup. Graphic designer? Help a fellow photographer edit his work.

Just make sure you have something solid to present to your clients to show off your skills.

Method #2: Choose Your Clients Carefully

"How can I compete for clients when other freelancers are offering their services at extremely low prices?"

A common myth most new freelancers fall victim to is believing that they can't compete with cheap freelancers just because of the pricing difference. If a client wants to get their job done for a cheap price, they will look for a cheap freelancer. That's what sites like Fiverr are made for. Avoid Fiverr and forget about those cheap clients. You're better off not working for them. But, if a client wants quality results, the price won't matter to them.

As a freelancer living in a developing country where the US dollar value is high, I had all the more reasons to offer a cheap price as a competitive advantage. Yet, I priced my services the same as a freelancer from the US. Why? Because I know the value of my skills, experience, and knowledge.

Price your services right and choose clients who will value your skills enough to pay your asking price.

For example, if you're working from a freelance site, you can look for the client's budget limit to see how much they are willing to spend on a project or check their hiring history to see what kind of freelancers they've worked with in the past.

Method #3: Learn How To Communicate

"Focus on making me comfortable with your communication skills. I'll pay 20x to work with a functional human."

Ben Vaello, a regular client on UpWork left that brilliant piece of advice as an answer to a question on Quora. Your communication skills matter more than anything. Don't frustrate your freelance clients with overly complicated words and technical explanations.

Instead, show your confidence. Write your client pitch and emails like you're talking to another human being. Be friendly. Use simple words. And keep it short.

Method #4: Keep Improving And Learn New Skills

Signup for online learning platforms like Skillshare and Udemy and start one or two courses in those sites. Try to watch a couple of those videos when you have free time. Heck just leave them playing in the background while you work.

It's easier to get comfortable thinking that what you already know is enough to make some money as a freelancer. But, you'll be surprised how little you know about your field after watching these courses.

Learning something new will not only help you learn new skills and earn more money, but it will also give you the confidence to talk passionately about different topics with your clients and flaunt your knowledge and expertise.

Make your clients think like "Wow, this guy sure knows what he's talking about."

Method #5: Provide A Solution, Not Advice

Each client posts a job on a freelance site hoping to solve a problem. Whether it's for creating an eBook, developing an app, or writing articles for their blog, they end up on sites like UpWork for a reason: To find someone good to get their work done right.

The least you can do before writing your pitch is to take a few minutes to carefully read their project description and hop on Google and do some research to figure out the best way to approach the job. And then you can write a unique pitch describing your take on their project.

For example, let's imagine that a client has posted a project for redesigning their website. If you're a web designer, you can visit their website and spend some time reviewing the site for its flaws and mistakes. Then you can write a pitch explaining how you plan on fixing those mistakes. This is a great way to show your enthusiasm and your love for what you do.

Method #6: If You Can't Beat Them, Join Them

Not all expert freelancers are jerks. Believe it or not, there are good freelancers out there who are willing to help out other new freelancers.

Send them a message, or connect with them on Twitter. Ask them how they land big clients or ask if they could throw you an extra job they have. You'll be surprised to see how kind some freelancers really are. If you couldn't find anyone, drop me an email. I'm always happy to help out a fellow freelancer.

Take Action!

Instead of complaining, find ways to stand out from the cheap and veteran freelancers. Offer more value for your price. Focus on delivering quality work and the clients will come knocking at your door.

Make a plan for figure out how you're going to make your services more valuable.

Lesson 18: How To Ditch UpWork And All Other Freelance Platforms

A while back, I reactivated my UpWork profile hoping to look for a job. I was going through a rough week with zero-clients and bills to pay. I had to explore every option.

It's been a while since I pitched for a job on UpWork. So, I refreshed my profile with new info and sent a proposal to a job. As usual, I didn't include my price in the first message. So, I received a reply from the client asking how much I would charge for the project.

Then I sent another message with my price. The client freaked out. He was furious and thought I was joking because apparently he's never seen anyone charge that much for writing an article before. I don't remember the exact price I pitched but I'm sure it wasn't what I'm charging right now.

That moment clearly defined the state of freelancing platforms for me. Most clients come to these sites to find people who do work for the cheapest price. Most of them don't care about quality, skill, and experience.

I was disappointed and left UpWork behind. Later I found a job from ProBlogger Jobs board and managed to get my financials back on track.

But, I learned a valuable lesson from that experience. I've had outgrown freelance platforms. The clients who used freelance platforms could no longer afford me. That's when I decided to completely quit freelance platforms.

No More Platform Fees

There are many benefits to ditching freelance platforms. One of the other big reasons that motivated me to quit freelance platforms is the platform fees that kept on changing.

UpWork is the worst example of a freelance site that keep increasing their platform fee for freelancers. The platform charges 20%. For what? Letting us browse a list of jobs?

We still have to propose to clients and win them over. And then put in the hard work to complete the project. And then, we lose 20% of our earnings on the platform fee?

It's not worth it!

When you're using job boards, you pitch to jobs directly via email. No more platform fees or processing fees. The payment comes directly to your PayPal.

Initiate Your Plan

Of course, freelance platforms provide a great foundation for beginners. They make it easier to find jobs when you're starting new. Use them until you gain some ground as a freelancer. It will be difficult to immediately quit using a freelance platform if you're too dependent on it. But, once you're comfortable, start taking your clients outside the platform.

If a client likes your work and shows interest to hire you again, contact them via email to let them know you also work outside the platform. Sites like UpWork prohibits sharing contact information in the platform chats, so look for the client company website to find their email.

When sending an email, you can offer a discounted price to get the client hooked. Since you're not paying a platform fee, you'll still be making more money.

Switch To Job Boards

Once you let go of freelancing marketplaces, start using job boards. These sites are more independent. You don't have to compete in bidding wars or register and maintain a profile or a rating. You can simply browse a job and apply for it directly via email.

You'll also notice that most jobs posted on freelance job boards usually come from reputable clients and offer higher pay as well. I've included a list of job boards in the freelance sites list included with the book. Be sure to check them out.

With enough experience and skill, you can completely depend on job boards to find quality work and maintain a stable income stream as a freelancer. This is how you can take control of your work, earnings, and your career.

Take Action!

Don't let a website or a corporation control your freelance career. Don't be too depended on UpWork or any other platform. Diversify and go beyond the freelance marketplaces.

Once you're ready, start making a plan to quit freelance sites for good.

Lesson 19: 10 Quick Ways For Finding Work Outside Freelance Platforms

Finding a freelancing gig without the help of a freelance site is not too hard. There are hundreds of job boards and dozens of methods you can use to find a work online. Here are just a few you can try.

Check The Careers Sections

When visiting websites, you may have noticed a link at the footer of most websites that says "We're Hiring" Or "Careers" or "Work With Us". These pages detail the positions currently available at a company. This means you can apply for these jobs. Visit websites related to your industry and check to see if they're hiring.

For example, if you're a marketer or a designer, you can try visiting a startup website like Canva to see if they have any job positions available at the moment. Companies like Canva has specific sections for remote jobs as well.

Behance & Dribbble Jobs

If you're a designer, you may have heard about Behance and Dribbble. They are two of the biggest networking platforms for creative professionals. But, did you know that you can also find jobs through these platforms?

Behance Joblist (https://www.behance.net/joblist) is the ideal place for finding jobs related to a wide variety of industries from copywriting to graphic design, photography and more.

Dribbble Jobs (https://dribbble.com/jobs) board is for designers. You'll find it always filled with jobs from reputable brands like Hotjar and Gameloft.

Simply search the list, find a job you like, and apply for it.

Write For A Blog

If you're a writer, you can instantly land a gig by writing for a blog. There are hundreds of blogs out there that pay people to write for their blogs. Some blogs even pay over $100 per blog post.

Of course, these are well-established blogs. You'll have to be a really good writer to land a gig on one of these sites. You can start by checking out these blogs that pay writers to publish blog posts.

- Listverse.com
- Travel Writer's Life.com
- Cracked.com
- Metro Planet.com
- Tutsplus.com
- SitePoint.com
- More (https://www.guestposttracker.com/blog/get-paid-to-blog/)

LinkedIn Jobs

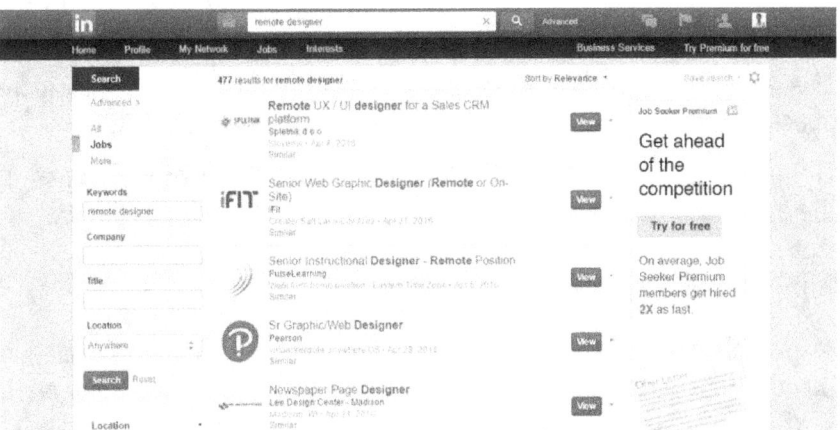

If you've got a professional looking profile on LinkedIn, then you should check out **LinkedIn Jobs** to find a quick freelance job.

To find a remote gig or a job near your location, just select your country from the list and type in the job position you're looking for. You can also use Posted Date and Job Function filters to narrow the search.

Set the **Location** to **Anywhere** and type **Remote** into the keyword field to find remote work.

Twitter Advanced Search

Every businesses has a Twitter account and when they're looking to recruit new employees, the first thing they do is post it on their Twitter. You just have to know how to search for them.

This is easy with **Twitter's Advanced Search** tool. In the keywords section, type in the title of the job you're seeking. For this example, I searched "designer" jobs.

Use a few keywords like "**Wanted**" or "**Hiring**" to make the search more specific. And type in several hashtags like #gig #freelancer #job.

Hit the **Search** button and voilà! You'll find hundreds of job listings in there.

Niche Job Boards

Many niche websites, magazines, and blogs also have their own little job boards. These sites usually have lots of quality job listings too. Here are a few sites you can check out:

- Smashing Jobs: For web and graphic design jobs.
- We Work Remotely: For design, marketing, and programming jobs.
- ProBlogger Jobs Board: For copywriting jobs.
- Freelance Writing Gigs: For copywriting jobs.

If you can't find anything helpful in those sites, just head over to Google and type these keywords into the search bar with the quotation marks **"jobs board" "web designer"** and hit enter. The results will show you plenty of sites with job boards. Replace "web designer" with your own keywords.

Browse Craigslist

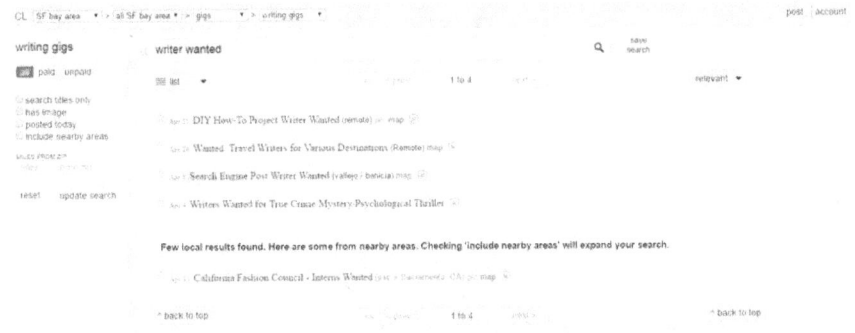

That's right! Craigslist is not all about rooms for rent and buying used car parts. It's also a great place for finding freelance jobs. Here, I'll show you how.

Step 1: Go to **Craigslist** and choose a country and then the city that you want to find a job in. (Major cities in the US have the most remote job listings).

Step 2: Then check the Jobs and Temp Jobs sections to find work related to your industry.

Step 3: Type in a keyword to find specific jobs like "**Wanted**" or "**Hiring**", just like how you did on Twitter.

Step 4: After finding a job, click on the **Reply** button to send an email to the person who posted the job.

Hacker News

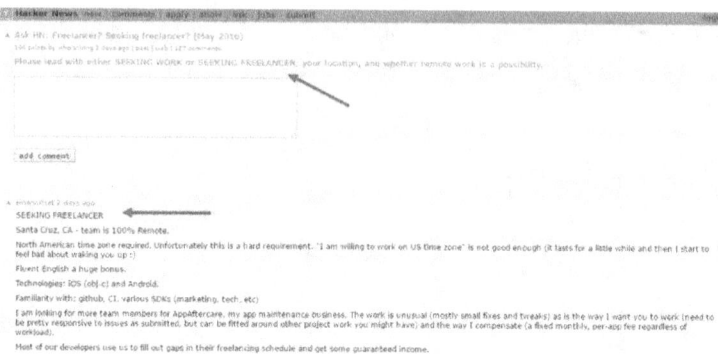

Whoishiring submissions on Hacker News can also be a great way to find work.

Pick a listing in there and post your information to attract potential clients. Or look for a job posted by a client. Use **SEEKING WORK** keyword to post your information or hit **Ctrl + F** on your keyboard and type **SEEKING FREELANCER** to find jobs posted by businesses.

Facebook Groups

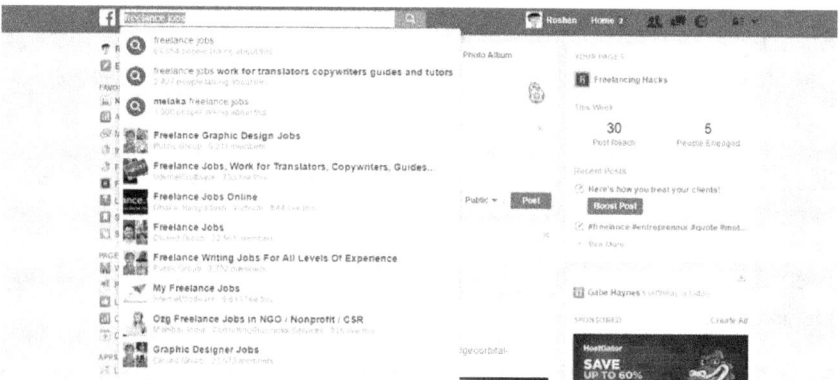

Facebook groups are still quite popular among both freelancers and business owners. Log in to your Facebook account and start searching.

Type in the keyword for your industry and find related groups under the search suggestions or click "**show all search results**" to find more groups. In this example, I typed in "**freelance jobs**" into my Facebook search bar and a bunch of massive groups popped up and they were filled with a lot of freelance gigs.

Search Job Forums

If you're new to freelancing, then you may not be familiar with job forums. Back in the old days, before oDesk and Elance, these job forums were the saviors that gave most freelancers paid jobs. Those sites are still active and hundreds of new job listings are published every day.

Just go over to a job forum and use the search bar to find a job. Here are a few job forum sites you can start with:

- **Gumtree.com**
- **Indeed.com**
- **Creative Planet Network.com**
- **Digital Webbing.com**

Take Action!

There's more than one way to find a job. Take a pen and paper and write down the many ways you can try to find a freelance gig. Try them one by one until you land a client.

Don't complain. Be willing to do the work!

Freelancing Secret #4 - The One Thing You Can Do To Get Repeat Clients

Imagine having to choose between two clients. One client offers a long-term contract for multiple jobs over the course of months. The other client offers a big payout for a short two week project, who would you pick?

Obviously, you would choose the first client because in the long term your payout will be higher than the second job and it will save you the trouble of having to look for a new client for a long time.

That kind of financial security is worth more than gold to freelancers. It's exactly why you should try to find retainer clients instead of completing one-off jobs. A retainer client will give you more work over a certain period of time. Sometimes months or years.

Most clients who hire you will always have more work to be done. But, their decision to hire you again will depend on how you make a first impression and how you deliver the project.

Go The Extra Mile

If there's one thing that makes a client fall in love with you and give you more work over and over again, that is how much effort you put into a project.

If you can find a way to deliver a project that surpasses a client's expectation it will help you leave a great impression of how much you care about your work and satisfying your clients.

If you're a freelance writer, you can create a unique header image to go along with your articles. If you're a web designer, include a mockup template or design an extra page for free. If you're a graphic designer, you can include a different variation of the design for free.

This simple extra step will help you cement a strong relationship with your client. A simple gesture will show how passionate you are about your work and it will show how you're different from other freelancers.

Find a way to go that extra mile and you will never have to struggle to find new clients ever again.

Lesson 20: How To Write An Effective Cold Email

Writing the perfect email is a skill you'll have to master if you want to leave freelancing platforms for good. Because, once you quit freelance sites, you will have to reach clients directly via email to propose for a job.

Whether you're sending an email to a client after reading their job posting on a job board or directly contacting a company, here are a few tips that will help you write the perfect cold email to get a conversation going and eventually land a client.

#1 Get Into A Positive Mindset

Before you even get into writing the email, you need to prepare yourself to be positive. There should be no begging, complaining, bragging, or any negative words in your email. Clients will be able to tell whether you're desperate for a job or truly interested in working with them just by reading your email.

Make sure you really want to work with this client. That you would love working for this company. That you are the perfect candidate for this job. And you can do incredible work with this project. Truly believe in it. And be positive that you are going to win this client. Have no doubt about it. Then you can start writing the email.

#2 Use A Template But Be Creative

Using a template will help you keep the proper structure in your email and also keep your email short and precise. No client will have the time to read a 1,000-word email, no matter how skilled you are.

You can use one of the email templates I've included with this book. However, avoid copy-pasting. Always write original emails with your own words.

#3 Find Their Needs And Personalize

Dig deep down into the company culture and find out where they are struggling and use that as fuel to write your pitch. For example, if you're a freelance writer, you can explore the company's blog to see what type of blog posts performed the best in the past. You can use a tool like Buzzsumo to get that job done.

Then you can figure out a way to create new content that's better than the most successful posts on their blog. If a blog post about 10 tips for starting a website is successful. Maybe you can write an article with 101 tips. Pitch that to your client.

First of all, the client will love the fact that you've spend that much time researching their company. Second, the client will see that you already have a plan to make their company blog better. You're hired!

#4 Email The Right Person

Before sending that email, just make sure you have the right person's email.

If you picked up the email from a job board, then you have nothing to worry about. But, if you're reaching out to a company, then you need to find the right person to get in contact with. Usually, it should be the hiring manager or even the CEO would do the trick.

Most websites have a page called "Our Team" where they showcase all their employees. That's the place you need to start looking.

Whatever you do, avoid sending cold emails using company website contact forms. You can use the contact form to ask for the email of the person in charge of hiring. But, don't send them the pitch.

#5 Show Your Worth

Here's a nifty trick you can use to get your client's attention.

Sometimes, approaching a client directly and asking for a job won't work. For example, if working with someone like Gary Vaynerchuk is your dream, then you shouldn't ask for a job straight away.

Instead, you can write an amazing blog post about him listing the key lessons people can learn from him. And, you can reach out to Gary to ask for an original quote to include in this blog post. Once published. Send him the link. Be casual and friendly. After a couple of weeks. Reach out to him. Show how many likes and views your article has received. And ask if he would like to see this type of posts on his own blog.

Take Action!

Cold emailing works. You just have to figure out the right angle to approach the client. Be creative and try to find new ways to write each new email. For a test run, try cold contacting your favorite entrepreneur right now. Send them an email admiring their work. See if you'll get a response. Don't be afraid. What's the worst that could happen?

Lesson 21: How To Pick And Manage The Right Clients

There will come a time when you have to decide between clients. Which one to keep and which one to drop. I had to face that problem couple of times. One time, I was approached by a reputable startup and invited me to join their content marketing team. I was delighted to join.

But, if I were to join their team, I would have to let go of one of my existing clients to free up space. This was a tough choice because I had already worked with my existing client for months. He was reliable and paid me on time.

On the other hand, I don't know much about this new client. Will they pay me on time? Will they like my work? Will I lose work after a few weeks?

This new client, however, offered to pay me a slightly higher rate. As a bonus, I will also get to learn how a startup content marketing team works. So, I let go of my old client and joined the new team.

It was one of the best decisions I've made.

It's About Quality, Not Quantity

When it comes to picking clients, you always have to consider their quality. It's not about how many clients you have or how many jobs they are offering you. It's about how much you're getting paid and what kind of value their work gives you.

This is also why I advise people to avoid platforms like Fiverr.

It's always worth waiting a month until you find a client who pays you $50 for writing an article than immediately signing a long term contract with a client who pays you $5 per article.

Drop Bad Clients

If a client is asking you to do too many revisions of your work. Always harassing you when giving feedback. Always pays you late. Then it's time to drop this client.

It can be difficult to let go of a client when you know he brings you money. But, a client who drains your mental and physical energy is not worth the hassle.

Focus on clients who encourage you and always say "great job", even while giving feedback. You will do great work when you're working with those clients. They are not too hard to find.

Always Look To Expand

As I've mentioned in my story earlier, there will come a time when you have to decide between clients. Your brain will tell you to always stick to the safe path and avoid risks. But, if you want to grow, you will need to follow your gut and take a risk sometime.

Ask yourself, where do you want to see yourself in 10 years? And will this new client help me in any way to get me closer to that goal?

Keep An Address Book

Don't mark those old clients as history just yet. You might need them someday.

Keep a list of emails of all the clients you've worked with in the past. This will come in handy in times when you're desperately in need of a job. This way you can reach one of those old clients and ask to see if they have an opening available instead of looking for new clients on job boards.

Building a career is not about settling down with the safest client. It's about finding the right clients who help you grow.

Take Action!

Don't settle for less. Learn to pick clients who help you grow and advance your career. And create an email address book for all your clients. It will come in handy.

Exercise 3 - Beyond Freelance Platforms

Test what you've learned so far.

Q1: Write a simple example message asking a testimonial from your client.

Answer:

Q2: What would you say to a client who asks for a free sample of your work?

  A: Yes, I will do it.

  B: I don't do free work.

  C: Offer to do the sample, but charge for it.

Answer:

Q3: Name 3 ways you can beat veteran and cheap freelancers.

Answer:

Q4: Name 3 ways you can find work outside freelance marketplaces.

Answer:

Freelancing Secret #5 - How To Be An Exceptional Freelancer

Imagine that you own an electric Tesla car. One day this car breaks down. You come across two technicians who claim to be able to fix it. One claims to be an expert on all kinds of vehicles from motorbikes to trucks and even airplanes. And the other claims to be a specialist that only works on Tesla brand electric vehicles. Who would you pick to fix your Tesla car?

The choice is obvious, isn't it? You want the best man to fix your car no matter how much they charge for it. You will choose the man who knows your vehicle and the brand well.

Don't Be A Jack Of All Trades

In the world of freelancing, this is pretty much the same.

When a client wants to develop an eBook on starting a website, he will hire the freelance writer who specializes in WordPress over all the other writers. If a client wants to hire a social media manager, he will choose the freelancer who already built a Facebook page with 10K followers. If a client wants to build a mobile-first website, he will hire the web designer who specializes in Bootstrap framework.

Specializing in a specific skill is a great way to guarantee a successful career. Whenever you come across a job that fits your skillset, you will be able to land that client without much effort. It's great to be a man/woman of many skills. I actually went through a series of phases. First, I did graphic design work, started a blog, then I wanted to be a freelance writer, then tried to be a web designer, then started a company, and then came back to being a writer again.

But, all those skills I've learned while pursuing those different paths have helped me to become a better writer. Now I get more jobs from web design and development related businesses because they're impressed by my knowledge.

While it doesn't hurt to learn multiple skills and expand your knowledge, you shouldn't try to be an expert of all skills. Instead, learn many but focus on one or two skills and try to master them. This will pay you well in the long run.

Invest In Yourself, Your Reputation, And Your Skills

Congratulations on reaching here! You're now fully prepared to start a career in freelancing and you already have a head start.

It took me over 6 years of hard work and making a lot of costly mistakes to learn everything that I've shared with you in this book. If I had these lessons when I first started my freelance career, things would've gone very differently.

I hope this guide will help you avoid the mistakes I've made and build an even more successful freelance career in a much shorter time.

Keep Improving Yourself

Even if you've completed a degree and consider yourself an expert in your field, don't stop learning. Follow online courses, read books, subscribe to blogs, and keep feeding your brain with more knowledge. It will only increase in value over time.

You Must Outwork Everyone Else

I can't guarantee how much money you'll earn as a freelancer. Because, it clearly depends on how much effort you're willing to put into your work and follow my advice. If you truly have a burning passion to become a freelancer, then follow my advice. You will eventually end up making more than $1K a month.

I created this book with 21 lessons and asked you to read 1 chapter per day. Because, I know it's hard to concentrate and finish a book within a short time. That's why I made it easier to digest.

However, it will take time for you to develop your skills and build reputation. Then you'll have to find clients and keep practicing your skills to truly make a profitable income.

The harder you work, more you will earn. Don't finish this book and expect clients to knock on your door. Work for it. And train yourself to outwork everyone else.

As my final piece of advice, I'll leave you with a quote from Elon Musk.

"If other people are putting in 40-hour work weeks and you put in 100-hour work weeks, you will achieve in 4 months what it takes them a year to achieve."

Epilogue

If you have any complaints, suggestions, or even need any help with anything related to freelancing, feel free to drop me an email -

roshan@freelancinghacks.com

I'm hoping to take your feedback and improve this book over time.

Also, join the private Facebook Group for exclusive content.

Facebook Page - https://www.facebook.com/freelancinghacks/

Twitter page - https://twitter.com/freelancehackz

Facebook Group - https://www.facebook.com/groups/293038821083100/

Email Template - For Developers

Hi **[Client's name]**,

My name is **[your name]** and I was just browsing your website **[name of the website]**. I've been using your online tool for several months now and I must say I really love how it allows users to **[mention a good feature about the tool]**.

The one thing that frustrated me was that I couldn't access your service on my phone. And I actually came up with a great design and a plan to develop an Android app for your service. If you're interested, I'd love to share some of the details.

By the way, I have some pretty good experience developing apps too, **[number]** years to be exact. My most recent work was **[link and name of an app]**. Check out my portfolio for more info **[link to your portfolio website]**.

Send a reply if you'd like to talk more.

Kind regards,

[Your email signature]

Email Template - For Graphic Designers

Hi **[Client's name]**,

I saw your job opening while browsing **[name of the website]**, are you still looking for a graphic designer to create your business logo?

I've been doing graphic design work for **[number]** years now and I also have experience working at an advertising agency as a lead designer as well. Just recently I designed a new logo for **[name of the company]**. You can see it at **[link to website]**.

Have a look at some of my previous designs on my portfolio at **[link to your portfolio]**.

I read through your job description and the business website and I already have a few good ideas for the logo design. If you could send in more details and the requirements I'd be happy to send over a few sketches of the design.

Kind regards,

[Your email signature]

Email Template - For Marketers

Hi **[Client's name]**,

I'm **[your name]** and I'm a content marketer. I noticed on **[name of the website]** that you're looking to outsource your social media marketing. I'd be happy to help you out with the process.

Social media and inbound marketing are two of my strongest suits. I recently helped a client grow their social media following to 10K likes on Facebook and Twitter **[include links to examples of your work]** within three months.

You can also visit my personal website to see some of my work. **[link to your portfolio]**

I see that your social media pages are not fully optimized for latest standards. I'd gladly do that for you in addition to putting together a content plan to promote your brand on your social media channels.

If you have a few minutes, I'd like to ask some questions regarding your targets and goals. Let me know if you'd like to schedule a Skype call.

Kind regards,

[Your email signature]

Email Template - For Web Designers

Hi **[Client's name]**,

I came across your job posting on **[name of the website]** where you said you're looking for a web designer to reconstruct your business website.

I've worked with a lot of great brands and small businesses over the past **[number]** years, including **[mention names of your previous clients with links to websites]**. They've praised my work as exceptional and reported back great increases in conversion rates and sales after the new website design.

You can check out some of my work on my portfolio at **[link to your portfolio]**.

I have a few ideas on how to approach your job on designing the website. If you're interested, I'd love to discuss more details.

Kind regards,

[Your email signature]

Email Template - For Writers

Hi **[Client's name]**,

My name is **[your name]** and I'm a freelance copywriter.

I just saw your job posting on **[name of the website]** and noticed that there's an opening for a blog article writer in your business blog.

I've been working online as a freelance writer for **[number of years]** years and I managed to help develop several great and successful blogs for my clients.

Not to brag, but I also have multiple articles published on popular authoritative websites such as **[mention and link to the websites]**. Have a look and see if my writing style fits your blog's strategy.

I understand that getting a lot of shares on social media is just as important as optimizing articles for search engines. And I use a handful of tools to make sure to target both those areas.

If you like, I can come up with some topics and ideas for great articles for your blog.

Kind regards,

[Your email signature]

70+ Websites For Finding Freelance Work

With this massive list of websites, you will never have to complain about not being able to find a job. Pick a site and apply for a gig.

Most Popular Platforms (High Competition)

Popular freelance platforms are often crowded with too many freelancers and are too competitive for beginners. Avoid these sites if you can.

#1 UpWork.com

Various types of jobs for all types of freelancers

#2 Freelancer.com

Jobs under multiple categories

#3 People Per Hour.com

Jobs for all types of freelancers. Hourly based pricing.

#4 99Design.com

For design related jobs.

#5 Guru.com

Various types of jobs.

#6 Toptal.com

Coding and software development related jobs.

#7 College Recruiter.com

For college students and recent graduates.

#8 Speedlancer.com

Deliver work in under a specified time.

#9 Envato Studio.com

Handpicked freelancers. Exclusive access.

#10 SimplyHired.com
Jobs from popular companies.

Niche Platforms & Job Boards (Low Competition)
Stick with niche freelance sites and job boards to increase your chances of landing a job.

#11 GoLance.com
New freelance platform. Low competition.

#12 AngelList (angel.co)
Remote freelance and full-time jobs posted by startups.

#13 Hired.com
With a profile on this site, the companies will come looking for you.

#14 Work Market.com
Best for sales and marketing related jobs.

#15 Crew.co
Web design and development jobs.

#16 Gigster.com
Coding jobs.

#17 RemoteOK.io
Remote jobs board with multiple categories.

#18 Liquid Talent.com
Jobs platform for developers and designers.

#19 Authentic.com
Content marketing related jobs.

#20 Github Jobs.com
Coding jobs for programmers.

#21 **Inbound.org**

Marketing and content writing jobs.

#22 **Landing.Jobs**

Web design and UXD jobs.

#23 **Proz.com**

For freelance translators.

#24 **Remotive.io**

Remote jobs from reputable companies.

#25 **Outsourcely.com**

New freelance platform. Low competition.

#26 **Problogger.com/Jobs**

Freelance writing jobs. Best for established writers.

#27 **Freelance Writing Gigs.com**

Freelance writing jobs for all.

#28 **Zeerk.com**

Similar to Fiverr. But low competition.

#29 **Twine.fm**

New and growing freelance platform.

#30 **CloudPeeps.com**

Another growing new freelance site.

#31 **People As A Service.co**

Freelance platform with low competition.

#32 **Talent Cupboard.com**

For students and recent graduates.

#33 **The Freelancer Club.co.uk**

UK-based freelance site for creatives.

#34 Jobs Outsource.com
For finding both online jobs and local jobs.

#35 Growth Geeks.com
Best for creatives.

#36 WP Hired.com
WordPress related jobs.

#37 GetACoder.com
Coding and software development jobs.

#38 Smashing Jobs.com
Design related jobs.

#39 Mashable Jobs.com
Tech related jobs.

#40 Krop.com
Job board for creatives.

#41 Working Nomads.co/jobs
Job board for various types of jobs.

#42 Coroflot.com
Design related jobs.

#43 StackOverflow.com/Jobs
Software development jobs.

#44 Dribbble.com/Jobs
Design related jobs.

#45 Behance.net/JobList
Design related jobs.

#46 WeWorkRemotely.com
Job board for various jobs

#47 **Hirable.com**
Various jobs.

#48 **OnSite.io**
Best for established freelancers.

#49 **Design Crowd.com**
Freelance design jobs.

#50 **Power To Fly.com**
Best for female freelancers.

#51 **Traction.com**
For freelance marketers.

#52 **Rev.com**
Transcription jobs.

#53 **CraigsList.org**
Various jobs.

#54 **Monster.com**
Various jobs.

#55 **Peer Hustle.com**
Find jobs based on your location.

#56 **LinkedIn.com/Profinder**
Be discoverable.

#57 **Design Hill.com**
Graphic design jobs.

#58 **Thumbtack.com**
Various jobs. Both online and offline.

#59 **Damongo.com**
Gig-based freelance site.

#60 **Juiiicy.com**
New site for designers.

#61 **Field Nation.com**
Find local jobs.

#62 **YunoJuno.com**
Only for New York and London based freelancers.

#63 **Just Answer.com**
Get paid to answer questions.

#64 **Aquent.com/Find-Work**
Marketing and creative jobs.

#65 **Tutor.com**
Online tutoring jobs.

#66 **FreelanceMap.com**
Tech related jobs.

#67 **Joomlancers.com**
Programming jobs.

#68 **Jobs.WordPress.net**
Jobs for WordPress developers.

#69 **Workhoppers.com**
Find local jobs.

#70 **Student Freelance.com**
For college students and graduates.

#71 **Scripted.com**
For bloggers.

#72 **Voice123.com**
For voice actors.

10+ Sites For Learning New Skills Online

Before you start your freelance career, it's important to polish up your skills and even learn a few new skills.

Here are the best sites for learning skills online.

#1 Skillshare.com

Classes in short videos to make it easier for you to learn in minimum time.

#2 Udemy.com

Various courses. Best to wait for a promotion if you want to buy courses for $10.

#3 edX.org

Courses from the world's top universities. It's free to audit. But you'll have to pay to receive certificates.

#4 Coursera.org

High quality courses from top universities and colleges. Free to audit.

#5 Lynda.com

Learn various skills from professionals. Monthly subscription.

#6 Tutsplus.com

Online courses for designers and developers.

#7 Udacity.com

High quality courses and micro degrees from reputable companies, including Google.

#8 Open.Edu

Open-source learning. Free courses.

#9 Alison.com

Online courses for learning different types of skills.

#10 Code Academy.com

Learn the basics of programming languages like, HTML, CSS, JavaScript for free.

#11 Khan Academy.org

Free online courses for learning various types of subjects.

#12 Code.org

Courses for learning to code.

#13 Degreed.com

A huge list of online learning sites for free courses.

www.ingramcontent.com/pod-product-compliance
Lightning Source LLC
Chambersburg PA
CBHW051321220526
45468CB00004B/1447